LETTERS

TO

DOCTORS

LETTERS

TO

DOCTORS

—•••—

Philo*Sophia: the Love of Wisdom

REVEREND C. EARLE CARPENTER

Union Hill Publishing
200 Union Hill Drive, Suite 200
Birmingham, AL 35209

www.richardesimmons3.org

1 2 3 4 5 6 7 8 9 10

Printed in the United States of America

DEDICATION

———•••———

This book is dedicated to my loving wife, Judy, who for 22 years cooked dinner on Monday nights for medical and dental students always with love and never a complaint. She not only pointed me to Christ but served by my side in ministry to our Lord for 60 years and counting.

TABLE OF CONTENTS

———•••———

FOREWORD

—•••—

By Dr. Joby O'Brien

I grew up in Birmingham, Alabama, and loved it so much that I never wanted to leave—with the exception of going to the University of Notre Dame for college. However, in 1988 I found myself moving to New Orleans for a General Practice Dental Residency at the VA Hospital. This was a momentous event for me because I had become a born-again believer after being raised Roman Catholic, and the irony was I was moving not only physically but spiritually as well. New Orleans is a hotbed of Catholicism, yet I would be looking for a Protestant church to attend.

I talked with a couple of locals who knew the churches in New Orleans, and on the first Sunday of July I left my apartment in Kenner and made the 20-mile journey through downtown New Orleans before I ended up at a small church on the West Bank called Berean Bible Church. I walked in during the Sunday School hour, and the host at the door pointed me to the correct room. I was terrified as I entered because the class had already started and all eyes were on me. The nice gentleman teaching (turns out it was the pastor) looked and asked who I was, and I replied, "I'm Joby O'Brien, and I just moved here from Birmingham." To my surprise he looked back at me and said, "My name is Larry Miller, and Earle Carpenter told me you were coming!" And such has been my relationship with Earle for over 40 years: fortuitous and God-directed.

Earle and Judy Carpenter have been a tremendous blessing in not only my life but the lives of my entire family. They have been with me during the highs and lows. In my junior year of dental school, I had noticed this older guy who was not a dentist hanging around with some of my classmates that I knew to be "the Christians." From the moment we met, Earle took me under his wing and taught me about being a believer in Jesus and a true disciple of Christ. I heard a speaker once say, "We all have someone on our hand." By that he meant there are usually four or five people who have had the most impact in our lives. A kind of Hall of Fame of those who have loved and given to us in our lives. Earle and Judy have been on "my hand" since 1987. Earle officiated the marriage of my wife, Iris, and me back in 1995. For a number of years, we were fortunate to minister with Earle and Judy as leaders for the young married couples of the Christian Medical Ministry of Alabama (CMMA). The Carpenters were always there to welcome and say a blessing over each of our four newborn children. They have been renamed

"Mama Judy" and "Papa Earle" as they have taken on the status of proxy grandparents to our kids.

Earle has also been an instrumental part of my life in the midst of difficult circumstances. He was there for me when my father passed away in 2008 and basically became a surrogate dad to me. For many years after that we met at Panera Bread on Fridays and Earle would spiritually pour into me. There have been difficult times when he had to confront me about sinful areas of my life but it was always convicting, uplifting, and restoring. He always embodies Proverbs 27:6, "The wounds of a friend are faithful."

Putting this book together has been a labor of love. I can't believe I am quoting Nick Saban (I'm not an Alabama fan at all—Go Irish and War Eagle!), but I heard him once say, "For every 'Thank you' comes an 'I owe you.'" God put this project on my heart because these lessons from God through Earle are too good to let them be forgotten. It has been fun to track down as many of these original newsletters as my colleagues and I could (we couldn't find them all), get them all on a digital format, and organize them. This book is my "thank you" for all of Earle's discipleship into my life. Thank you, Earle —I owe you and I love you!

INTRODUCTION

———•••———

Life is made up of various kinds of philosophy. What is a philosophy? We can begin to understand what it is by looking at the subtitle of this book, Philo*Sophia. It is broken into two words: Philo, which is the Greek word for love (for example, in the name of the U.S. metropolis of Philadelphia, which means "the city of brotherly love"), and Sophia, which means wisdom. In our numerous years of ministry, my wife, Judy, and I have strived to become...lovers of wisdom. Wisdom that only God can give, and in turn our desire has been to bring to doctors the love of wisdom that can only come from Jesus.

As I walked into surgery with Dr. Evan Zeiger, whom I was shadowing for the day, another doctor knew the doctor I was with and looked at me and said, "Who are you?" I just responded, "I'm a doctor to doctors." Back in 1982, the Alabama Impaired Physicians committee, local dentists, and numerous supporters from Campus Crusade for Christ reached out to me and asked me to come start a ministry to doctors. They had seen the devastation physicians were experiencing in their personal lives and how it was destroying them and their families. Dentists and psychiatrists led all professions in rate of suicide. Physicians doubled the general population in addictive behaviors such as alcoholism and drug abuse. Doctors were hurting. As one doctor told me, "After 20 years I built my practice on the ladder of success...but it was on the wrong wall."

As a vision of local dentists and physicians, we started the Christian Medical Ministry of Alabama (CMMA) on June 1, 1982. Since I had no previous experience in the medical field, it took time to acclimate and learn what doctors need and the demands on them. As it has been said, if you are going to speak to the culture then you need to know the language of the culture. It became apparent that so many doctors don't have a counselor or a friend. My father used to tell me, "Find a man's needs...and meet them and you will have a friend." I learned how to spend time with them on rounds through the hospital, in surgeries, in their office, and even in their homes. Proverbs 18:24 says, "A man that has friends must show himself friendly: And there is a friend that sticks closer than a brother." Spending time with them in their world became the most effective way to show the love of Christ to these servants. I learned to listen, not give an agenda. Because they are so busy, I learned how to give a two-and-a-half-minute Bible study on an elevator ride. No matter how gifted a surgeon or smart a doctor, a deep-felt need was always discovered when I asked, "How is your family doing?"

We trust our doctors to take care of us when we are sick or injured, as well as in times of wellness. We never take into account that our healthcare providers may be hurting as much as we are, just in different ways. There are three parts of what makes our person: body, soul, and spirit. Unfortunately, if we don't know Jesus as our personal savior our spirit is dead. It regenerates upon our conversion. The best doctors are the ones who can minister to the whole patient: body, soul, and spirit.

For 37 years Judy and I have ministered to these wonderful healthcare providers and their families. We have celebrated with them in triumph and grieved with them in loss and sorrow. I have been a part of observing hundreds of surgeries, many weddings (and premarital counseling), numerous baptisms, and unfortunately too many funerals. But through it all God has blessed me with being able to be a friend and a doctor to doctors.

This book is a series of the devotions that I wrote in monthly newsletters to these doctors, their families, and the prayer partners in our CMMA network over many years as we ministered to these wonderful servants. I have noticed that any subject involving Christianity can be put into any of four categories: Walk, Warfare, Word, and Worship. With that in mind, each of the devotions has been sorted into one of these four topics. It is my hope that the Lord will use these to encourage you to seek wisdom. May you grow in your love of wisdom! If you love wisdom, you are loving Jesus...for now—for eternity. Philo*Sophia.

Earle

CHAPTER ONE

WALK

—•••—

MUST PRIDE HAVE A FALL

These six things the Lord hates; indeed seven are an abomination to Him; a proud look (the spirit that overestimates himself and underestimates another)... Proverbs 6:16-17

Are you trying to fly without strings? Mark it down on your scratch pad: Whenever you are in conflict with someone else, "pride" is heavily involved. Pride makes a god of self. It makes you impatient when someone contradicts your opinion or desires.

Symptoms diagnosed are:

- Quarreling over rights

- Competition

- Rivalry

Any 'slight' could be proof positive that you have the outcroppings of pride. Pride covets praise and caters to applause.

It is the nature of freedom that it has fences and boundaries. True freedom is not to be cut loose from the strings of life but to be enslaved to Jesus. What a paradox! Pride resists change even when friends lovingly point the way. Pride resists being taught. Winston Churchill said:

"We all want to learn, but we all hate to be taught."

Pride will produce burnout. Are your days exhausting? Are you running out of time and energy? Are you running on empty? Are you tired of giving...serving...and expending what time and energy you have, whether it be at the hospital or home? Pride says, "I want to know more, do more, be a 100 percenter, control all." With this mindset, people become problems to be avoided, phone calls are intrusions, and unexpected guests are intruders. I know recently I have felt I cannot handle another heartache...need...hurt... even another person. I want to run away, build a wall, be a hermit. This hurts, but I have concluded I am prideful. What is the answer to burnout? Dealing with pride is a significant first step. Do we want to control or be controlled? Pride will resist being controlled.

Is it possible that we are trying to **"fly without strings,"** chafing at the strings of life...that God has given us?

"Ah! Foolish kite, though hadst not wing.
How couldst thou fly without a string?" —John Newton

Cut loose the strings of pride—embrace the strings of Jesus that allow you to fly!

———•••———

BE DISTINCTIVE

One of the distinguishing qualities of the person of God…is that of being distinctive. We are to be different, whereas the lifestyle of the "Twenty-first Century" politically correct is "blend in."

You shall not sow your vineyard with two kinds of seed… you shall not plow with an ox and a donkey together; you shall not wear a material mixed of wool and linen together. Deuteronomy 22:9-11

The book of Leviticus has to do with regulations for "worship." The book of Deuteronomy has regulations for "work and walk." Leviticus has to do with our "worship" of God; Deuteronomy has to do with our "walk" before mankind.

Why did he say not to plow with an ox and donkey together? These two animals have a different gait…a different height…and in light of the Scriptures it indicates that the first was considered a clean animal, the other unclean.

One of my favorite quotes Dr. Bill Bright used to say when I was on Crusade staff in 1969 was, "You can not hunt with the hounds and run with the rabbits." You have to choose! James says that a double-minded man is unstable in all his ways. You cannot ride two horses going in opposite directions or you will develop a split personality! By nature, the ox and the donkey are entirely different.

The prohibitions are for our blessing and not to be a burden. Search the Scriptures as the authoritative voice that will end your weary quest for a reliable guide for conduct. When God says not to do something it is for our provision and our protection. God's words are merciful guideposts. God has never sought to instruct us to lay weight upon our backs but rather to give light to our eyes.

Do not allow yourself to be governed by mixed principles. God is interested in purity of life. Becoming loose in your heart attitude soon results in becoming lax in your daily walk!

The Apostle Paul relates what was revealed in Deuteronomy to the Corinthian Christians:

> ***Do not be unequally yoked with unbelievers—do not make any alliances with them or come under a different yoke with them. For what partnership have right-living and right-standing with God with iniquity and lawlessness? How can light fellowship with darkness? What harmony can there be between Christ and Belial or what does a believer have in common with an unbeliever?***
>
> 2 Corinthians 6:14-15

This passage may be interesting, but it is the application that seems to be so difficult. Certainly, it is indicative in marriages. How else then could its application be applied?

> *"We do not need to succeed… the way the world*
> *succeeds but to fail…the way the Savior failed."*

God always operates out of principle, and soon after comes the promise.

> ***So come out from among unbelievers, separate yourself from them, says the Lord. Touch not any un-clean thing [principle]. Then I will receive you kindly and treat you with favor. I will be a Father to you, and you will be my sons and daughters [promise].***
>
> 2 Corinthians 6:17

> *"Obedience to God's will is not always convenient, but it is always profitable!"*
> —Bruce Wilkinson

Be distinctive for a reason. Godly success is distinctive…do not settle for less!

—•••—

OPEN THE WINDOW

For the love of Christ controls us… 2 Corinthians 5:14

Most doctors want to control everything versus being controlled by anything. A carpenter who as he was enlarging a window was accosted by the remark, "Ah! I see you are giving them more light." "No" was the reply. "I am not giving them more light; **I am giving them more window."**

Johannes Tauler in the 14th century said:

> *"Why blame the sun for not shining into the dwelling, when thou has closed the window? Open the shutters, and then it will enter in all its glory, and spread warmth around."*

More Window! More light—of the love of Christ, like a pressing crowd without and a burning fever within—presses and fires the truly Christian person.

"Control" means as a stream comes to a cliff it is pressed, forced through. The throng of people surrounding Christ pressed in and crushed Him. If the love of Christ is an inspired force within and a protected environment without, we shall know that the Christian life is a love-inspired life. The love of Christ is the only love that has no alloy of self, nor dross of unholy passion in the pure flame of His affection.

When Christ loved, He sacrificed. Love, like the sun shining in its warmth, continually gives itself to warm action—unlike mere sentiment, which, like the moon, is cold and barren. When the woman touched the hem of Christ's garment, the life in Him coursed through the whole of her being; so the love of Christ, when His love is known, causes the one who knows that love to sacrifice too. Paul was willing to sacrifice because the love of Christ controlled him.

I have seen many people sacrifice in the medical/dental field. For some it truly is because Christ controls them; for others…?

What a person is…gives value to what he does as seen in 1 John 3:17: "But if anyone has the world's goods and sees his brother in need, yet closes his heart against him, how does God's love abide in him?" To say well yet act ill, to plan yet not perform, to have a benevolent face yet no helping hand proves one hard, hollow, and selfish. Love is not like this. Love acts. It sees the need and supplies it; it is careless about its own comfort, but is careful about the comfort of others. Love weeps with the sorrowful, lifts the faint, heartens the discouraged, brightens the depressed, cheers the despondent.

Love does not patronize…it provides. Love provides a fire for the cold body, a bed for the destitute, a meal for the hungry, a warm heart for the rejected. Our heart's affection must be lit by and fed with the fuel of His love.

A lunatic, on one occasion, was found sitting at a table with an empty plate before him, holding a knife and fork. He made a pretense of eating. A friend asked him, "What are you doing?" "I am going through the 'motions'" was the reply. That lunatic may be saner than some sane people who imagine that the observance of outward things is of any consequence unless the inward realities are known.

Is Christ's love a power in your heart and life? Does it move and mold you? If not…why not? Seek that love. Seek Him who is the living expression of the love of God and then you will be able to say with Paul, "The love of Christ controls us."

Why don't you **open the window** of your soul and let the light of His love come in?

———•••———

TOUCH

"And a woman who had had a discharge of blood for twelve years, and who had suffered much under many physicians, and had spent all that she had, and was no better but rather grew worse. She had heard the reports about Jesus and came up behind Him in the crowd and touched His garment. For she said, 'If I touch even His garments, I will be made well.'" Mark 5:25-28

Is touching…important to you? Haven't you wanted someone to touch you, to hug you? Touching is often the way to confirm verbal expressions of love in interpersonal relationships. Kids thrive on touch!

She lived with a bleeding uterus for twelve humiliating years. She is labeled "unclean" by the Rabbis: unable to touch others or to be touched. Ostracized by the synagogue. Orphaned by society. Put out on the city streets or shoved down the steps, she has pleaded. She has prayed. For twelve agonizing years, God has been silent. Her downcast eyes show she is self-conscious, ashamed, and afraid.

With her having a bleeding uterus, anyone can guess what kind of sin she committed. "Sexual, no doubt" is the whispered innuendo. Trudging from doctor to doctor, she tried to find a place to lay her burden down. She spent all she had, she got worse, and she is now desperate. With her being out of money, the doctors finally admit there is nothing they can do for her. Her life is ebbing away. She is anemic…pale…and very, very, tired.

Every illusion she had about life is shattered. Suffering has a way of doing that. Her suffering had whisked dreams of family and children into little, broken piles.

But…she hears stories of another Physician who charges no fee, who asks for nothing in return, who has no hidden agenda. She begins to think…certainly if I can find Jesus and touch the fringe of His garment, I will be made whole.

So with this thin thread of faith, this frail needle of a woman stitches her way through the pressing crowd. Many are curious and eager; some are desperate too.

This desperate woman pushes her empty hand through a broken seam in the crowd and, for a fleeting moment, grabs the corner of His garment. Jesus is pulled back by the grasp of her faith. Power leaves Him to surge through the hemorrhaging woman, and immediately she feels the rush of her youthful health returning! In the flood of those feelings, she releases her grasp…swept away by the crowd.

Jesus does not let her get away. Her touch was different. That stopped Him in His tracks. Who touched Me?

"How ready Jesus is to respond
To the hands of outstretched faith."

Jesus finds her and reads the whole, sad story of the last twelve years. He sees isolation…introspection…insecurity.

The crowd blurs in the watery edges of her eyes. For one intimate moment, she sees only Jesus…He sees only her; face to face…Physician and patient.

Her needs were so great that fear did not paralyze her to touch, so that she could be touched.

"The chains of love are stronger than the chains of fear." —William Gurnall

Thank Jesus…now…for seeing every hemorrhage in your life through merciful eyes that understand and have a willingness to minister to your suffering.

Are you in emotional/physical pain? Why don't you reach out…and touch Him?

He "touched" you on the Cross. He is waiting.

———•••———

POWER

"My message and my preaching were not in persuasive words of wisdom, but in demonstration of the Spirit and of power that your faith should not rest on the wisdom of men but on the power of God." 1 Corinthians 2:4-5

What does your faith rest on? The wisdom of men or the power of God? Note that Paul says his message, which is his content, and his preaching, which is his communication of that content, were demonstrations of the Spirit of God and of power. God's power, thoughts, and ways stagger the imagination!

When God wants to do something, He is unsurpassed. When He makes an ocean, no man can fathom it; when He makes a mountain, no man can measure or scale it; when He makes flowers, there is no duplication among the billions of them.

God is not restrictive! His peace is like a river and passes all human understanding. His joy is unspeakable. His supply is without limit, and He gives and gives and gives. His grace has no sides or bottom, and the top has been left off. His wisdom is unsearchable! His strength is unexcelled; His salvation, unfathomable!

God is not just another god. He is the One and Only. God is not just another lord, He is the Lord of Lords. There are many gods that people might profess, which really are not gods: Buddha, Mohammed, Confucius, false religions, but there is only one Elohim...the Strong One. Only one Jehovah...the Living One. Only one Adonai... the Master. Only one El Shaddai...the Satisfier. The message of our ministry is not the wisdom of men but the **power of God.**

"Now unto Him who is able to do exceedingly abundantly above all that we ask or think, according to the power that works within us, to Him be the glory in the church and in Christ Jesus to all generations forever and ever. Amen." Ephesians 3:20-21

—•••—

POTS

"When you go through deep waters and great trouble, I will be with you. When you go through rivers of difficulty, you will not drown! When you walk through the fire of oppression, you will not be burned up, and the flames will not consume you." Isaiah 43:2

Waters…rivers…fires…flames. Enough to stop any of us!

Do you feel like you are passing through a deep and dark, overwhelming tunnel? God tells us circumstances might seemingly stop His people, but God promises you a way through. We don't bypass, but we go through! Why is that? Trials and difficulties are not to be evaded…but encountered. We don't run from, but we run with God's sustaining grace…through them. That is how you will know His sufficiency, at the end of your sufficiency.

Since the omniscient God knows the end as well as the beginning, He promises to bring you through, whether you are faced with a Red Sea, as Moses, or you're in the firey furnace, as Daniel. Their clothes did not even have the burnt smell! Whatever God says…believe it!

In 2 Corinthians 4:7-8, Paul says we are…

POTS
"We possess this precious treasure in Earthen vessels that the exceeding greatness of the power may be shown of God and not of ourselves."

We are "pots" to contain the glory of God, which is the light of the glory of God that is seen in the face of Jesus Christ.

…PRESSURES
"We're pressed on every side by troubles, but we aren't crushed or broken.
We are perplexed, but we don't give up and quit.
We are hunted down, but God never abandons us.
We get knocked down, but we get up again and keep going."

Sound familiar? We are Pots who are under Pressure for one reason: to show God's power.

"We always carry around in our body the death of Jesus, so that the

life of Jesus may also be revealed in our body." 2 Corinthians 4:10

There it is. Resurrection life is to be shown by our being Pots...under Pressure.

Through the waters...not alone...for purifying.
Through the rivers...not swamped...for pressure.
Through the fires...not harmed...for purging.

Reality hurts. The revelation of Jesus explains that the Holy Spirit enables us to proclaim the light...of the knowledge...of the glory of God of the face of Christ.

Did Isaiah say why this happens to you? "I traded their lives for yours because you are precious to me and honored and I love you. Do not be afraid for I am with you" (v. 4).

Isn't it wonderful to be loved in the midst of the pressures, **from the gutter most to the utter most?**

---•••---

WAITING

Waiting on Him...is always worth the wait!

"Blessed is the man who listens to Me...watching daily at My gates... waiting at the post of My doors." Proverbs 8:34

Blessed and happy is the person who takes time out for inaction. Nothing to do but to think.

Listening, watching, and waiting. Could you get apart in solitude so you can listen to His voice...watch His movements...and wait for His directions? Nothing to do but to be!

Life seems to be a daily cycle from crisis...to calm...to complacency...and then back to crisis, urgency, jitters again. Chaos instead of calm.

The **heart** is hungry until it feeds on the Bread of Life.
The **mind** is restless until it rests in the Father.
Your **will** is the guardhouse until He takes over supreme authority.
Your **love** yearns and lusts, seeking something to fasten upon...until it touches

God and clings in peace to Him.

Can you have a handful of quietness in the midst of clinic, call, schedule, complaints, and children?

Quietness—you must practice it to feel and enjoy it.

A calm spirit is like putting tobacco on the bee bite: It takes away the irritation and pain although the puncture remains.

The majority of us know nothing about waiting. **We don't wait; we endure.** Waiting means that we go on in the perfect certainty of God's goodness—no fear or doubts.

A man's patience is tested by three things: God, himself, and other people. An apt illustration is that of a bow and arrow in the hands of an archer. God is not aiming at what we are, nor is He asking our permission. He has us in His hands for His own purpose, and He strains to the last limit... then when He lets it fly, the arrow goes straight to **His goal.**

Most religious people are so busy with spreading and defending Christianity they have little time and less inclination for quiet meditation. Journals, books, Christian endeavors, professional priorities, and amusements so crowd our lives that people need deep inner resolution and planning to get a clear space to be quiet and listen to God.

It's not enough to think, to meditate, or to muse! Happy is the person who **hears** God, who **watches** at the Lord's gates, and who **waits** at His door.

Be still...and let God speak. **It's worth the wait.**

—•••—

BE IN THE NOW

Do you have fears of the future?

Do you live with past regrets...the if only's?

Do you live in the present moment?

It's the only option we have... live now!!

> *"So don't worry about tomorrow for tomorrow will bring its own worries. Today's trouble is enough for today."* Matthew 6:34

Back in 1998, when we were co-sponsors with Dr. Jack Carter of the Brennan Manning Conference "Living with the Beloved," Brennan gave me critical advice Saturday afternoon. As I went to pick him up at the hotel, he said God had impressed upon him a message…for me personally. He said, "Don't let anything worry you; don't let anything discourage you. Live in the present moment. Remember only things God does endure."

Imagine—expecting me not to worry about the future or continually rehearse the "if only's" of my life whether ministry, personal life, or family failures. **Imagine—living in the present moment!** Brennan told a story of a man that was being chased by a lion. He came to the edge of a cliff, and as he looked down 450 feet, he saw jagged rocks. But the lion was coming from behind. In the providence of God, he looks to the right, and there is a tree with a rope tied to it. He grabs the rope and shimmies down. He looked down and saw the jagged rocks below, the things in the future. He looked back up at the roaring lion…of his past.

Two mice began to gnaw on the rope. Then right in front of him in the crevice of a rock, was the most beautiful, biggest, reddest strawberry he had ever seen. As he munched on the strawberry, he said, **"Thank you, Abba, for providing for me… in this moment."**

Will you join me in living in the present moment? **"In thy presence is fullness of joy, and at your right hand are pleasures for evermore"**

(Psalm 16:9). Jesus is present in your presence.

Once I found this poem at a silent retreat in Cullman, Alabama sponsored by Emmaus Walk:

> "I was regretting the past and fearing the future. Suddenly the Lord was speaking:
> 'My name is…I AM.'
> When I live in the past with its mistakes or regrets, it is hard. I AM…is not there.
> 'My name is not I WAS.'
> When you live in the future with its problems and fears, it is hard. I AM…is not there.
> 'My name is not I WILL BE.'
> **When you live in this moment, it is not hard.**
> **'My name is…I AM.'**

To successfully live in the present moment is to walk by the enabling power of the

Holy Spirit. He will enable, equip, and encourage you to face your "present" situation with Joy. Jesus is here. He is available. He is listening, loving, and enabling you to live a supernatural life in the "present" moment. **Eat strawberries... with me!**

BE IN THE NOW.

—•••—

THE PRESENT MOMENT

When do you think you are successful in living? In the past, future, or present moment?

God Is No Where...or Now Here

Is God Now Here with you? Are you living in a present moment? A missionary who was being chased by a lion in Africa came to the edge of a cliff. What does he do? In the Providence of God, he sees a rope tied to a tree. Grabbing the rope, he shimmies down, and he sees 450 feet below the ragged rocks. He looks back up and sees the roaring lion. At that very moment in front of him, he saw a big red, juicy strawberry coming out of the edge of the cliff and said, "Oh, my Abba, thank you for the strawberry." And he ate the delicious strawberry!

The point—you will concentrate on either the lions of the past or the jagged rocks of your future. If so, you will also miss those luscious strawberries in the present!

People coming into medicine live a When, Then life.

> ***When...***I get into medical school
> ...I get into my 3/4-year clinicals
>   ...I find a residency
>   ...I get a practice
>   ...I get established
>   ...I get enough to retire
> ***Then...***I will investigate Christ or grow.

When will you live? We have 168 hours a week to spend, to gamble or experience a life of fruitful, happy, and Holy present moments!

"Teach us to number our days, and recognize how few they are. Help

us to spend them as we should." Psalm 90:12

Are you caught in a time squeeze? Do you feel harassed and swamped? Moses' challenge is the hardest "to number our days." We can know the status of our stocks, our mortgages, and practice income, and yet the most valuable asset is flying away…time.

"I have been crucified with Christ. It is no longer I that live, but Christ who lives in me. And the life I now live in the flesh I live by faith in the Son of God, who loved me and gave himself for me." Galatians 2:20

The word **now** is very annoying. If only Paul had said, "This is the kind of life I'm going to live. Or even after I'm dead in heaven. Down here, I'm encompassed about with sicknesses, pressures, pains." But he did not. He said, **"Now"** the life which I **now** live in the flesh, i.e., the present life we experience and others see. Are you living in the past? Our present enjoyment of God's grace is apt to be checked by the memory of yesterday's sins and blunders. Our future focus can bring us current fears. Jesus is the God of the "present moment" who did not say He was or will be but said, **"I am that I am."**

All that He is and all that you need are met in your thirst for drinking deeply at the well of living water in the present moment. The deeper you go, the sweeter it gets.

All we have is the "present moment." The only question is…are you going to be a straw person paralyzed by the future and past or are you going to eat strawberries?

———•••———

CONTENTMENT

Have you ever decided when you will be satisfied? Solomon has "painted" reality in Ecclesiastes 6. The paradox is that God gives a person wealth and honor so his soul lacks nothing of all he desires. But God may not empower him to eat from them. This is vanity!

> Children:…
> > Long Life…
> > > Hard Work…
> > > > …Wisdom

To overcome his frustration and despair, Solomon tried to add things to life that had potential of bringing him true happiness. First, he mentions that he had **many children** in hopes of finding satisfaction. He found his persistent inability to enjoy the fruit of his family. He thought he would have been better if he had been the victim of a miscarriage (v. 3). Why? He said the miscarriage "comes in futility, goes into obscurity and its name is covered in obscurity. It never sees the sun and it never knows anything" (v. 4-5a).

Since parenthood proved to be an inadequate solution for dissatisfaction, Solomon second considers **adding more years** to his life (v. 6). But he concludes that even a two-thousand-year life span would be miserable if one does not enjoy good things. He observes the individual who lives only a few years and the individual who lives many years. Both end up in the same place—the grave. So, what benefit is there for living a long life?

Solomon next reflects on his attempt of using **hard work** to relieve his depression. But that did not work either. His soul was not satisfied.

"Intensified labor will not bring contentment to an empty life."

Then he thought of a **good education**, practical discernment. Can it accomplish what the other things couldn't? Solomon answers, "No, for what advantage does the wise man have over the fool?" (v. 8)

The bottom line is **"What the eyes see...is better than what the soul desires"** (v. 9a). We need to stop dreaming about what we don't have and be content with what we do have.

Does life seem futile? It does to all of us at times. When we become frustrated, bewildered, or discontented, we often dispute with God. OUT OF GRACE, He tolerates our contentious spirits and lovingly seeks to persuade us to stop fighting Him and start trusting Him. Will you do that?

Are you fearful about the future? None of us knows what our future holds! However, Jesus Christ has assured us that if we build our lives on His word and act on His counsel, we will be like a "wise man who built his house upon the rock. The foolish man built upon the sand. The same winds blew and rains flooded. On which foundation does your life rest—the Rock or sand? Your answer reveals your source of contentment and your ultimate destiny—heaven or hell.

"The sight of the eyes is better than what the soul desires." What do you see in front of you that you could trust for contentment? Everybody lives in two tents:

Discontent or Content.

———•••———

PLEASURE OR PAIN

Nothing is born without pain. Having taken "call" in OB/GYN rounds, I have viewed the presence of pain in the midst of the physical birth process. The mother's joy erupts and pain moves to the background as the reality of birth is enjoyed.

When we are "born again," there is no more pain to us than at our natural birth. We are born by His pain into the realm where our Lord lives. The pain of God is graphically exhibited on Calvary. The birth of God's Son came with joy, overshadowed by the despair of death; but thirty-three years later it resulted in the joy of resurrection, three days after the despair of death.

We have to learn to take pain and weave it into the fabric of our lives. **If there were no pain, there would be no semblance of pleasure.** Dr. Paul Brand uses the illustration of leprosy patients. They burn their hands in fires because they do not experience any pain. Since they do not receive this "signal" of pain, their extremities become damaged. They would welcome pain…for it would protect!

Ecclesiastes teaches that wholesale devotion to "pleasure" paradoxically leads to a state of utter despair. We may start chasing pleasure as an end in itself and along the way lose sight of Who gave us the good gifts of taste, beauty, or even sexual excitement.

How do you live in the midst of pain…expecting pleasure? You live by faith. God does not want us to live by fear but by faith. Fear of pain in the past or future can cripple us. On one hand, fear can make us defensive; on the other, it can make us rush forward for fear of not being "with it." Nothing done under the influence of fear can bear the fruit of the Spirit.

Think of Jesus. He was not intimidated by public opinion, by what "others might think." Jesus kept His distance from the expectations and judgment of authorities who thought themselves to be respectable. When Jesus embraced Zacharias and the pain of his rejection, He did not look around fearing what people might think. He was neither afraid of their rejection nor concerned about stepping on toes.

"The expectation of others often acts as a subtle controlling pressure on our behavior."

The crowd does not take kindly to nonconformity. Doesn't the fear of ridicule paralyze us more effectively than flat-out opposition? Can you think of situations in which you have run from the pain of rejection—praying with a patient, not overbilling when it could be done, avoidance of going home to be with a rebellious teenager or a combative spouse?

Rejoice today that Jesus has taken the pain of sin so you can have the pleasure of a very vital and dynamic living relationship with God as a Father. Cry out to Him, **"Abba, Father"!!** That is a pleasure of life no one can block or take from you.

People in pain often try to pay for their sin, which has already been paid for by Jesus. Because of pride, they do not humble themselves to obey what they know God wants them to do—for the husband to love his wife as Christ loved the Church or for the wife to render a submissive spirit to the husband as unto the Lord. If we keep doing it "my way" we live in pain. If we do it "His way" we live in pleasure.

Pain or pleasure…which one will you choose?

—•••—

VISION

A great deal of life completely lacks vision—no vastness, bigness, or color. We are like people in the bottom of a well looking up. All we see is a little patch of blue sky. Our vision is microscopic; it should be telescopic. **THINK BIG!**

Not only does vision give perspective, but it gives focus. What gives you myopia… short-sightedness? **Unbelief** is the most active thing on earth; it is negative on God's side, not on ours. Unbelief is a worrying, fretful, annoying, questioning, self-centered spirit. Belief stops all this and lets God work.

"As far as I know, I've given up everything to the Lord," said a physician who was distressed because she did not have the joy and peace that she saw in others. "Perhaps you have given up everything except your unbelief," was the reply of a servant of Christ.

What does unbelief do? **Unbelief hinders the Lord in His working.** Christ could not accomplish much in His own hometown because of the townspeople's unbelief (Matthew 13:58). Unbelief hinders the operation of grace; it not only blights the soul but binds the hands of the Savior. Unbelief shuts out the light of God's benefits by putting up the shutters of its own willful way.

Unbelief shuts out blessing. Unbelief is always troubled with a short memory. The

Israelites, at the edge of the Promised Land, did not go in. Why? They could not enter because of unbelief (Hebrews 3:19). They forgot the mighty works of deliverance God had already done for them. The Israelites looked at things from man's standpoint that magnified the wrong things. If they had viewed things from God's viewpoint, they would have found that instead of being grasshoppers in the sight of the giants, the giants were grasshoppers in His sight!

Unbelief keeps blessing back from others. The reason the Disciples could not cast the demon out of the young boy was because of their unbelief (Matthew 17:20). So, if faith brings blessing, the opposite is also true...unbelief keeps it back. The man on the pallet was healed for faith's sake, the faith of the four men who brought him to Christ; the centurion's servant was restored for the faith's sake of the centurion. The daughter of the Syrophoenician woman was healed for faith's sake of the mother. Belief is like Esther. It comes into the presence of the King and secures blessing for its kin. **Unbelief is like Haman...**it brings devastation and distress to others.

> *"He who has a program without a vision is a worker.*
> *He who has a vision without a program is a dreamer.*
> *He who has a vision and a program is a conqueror!"*
> —Dr. Howard Hendricks

The vision of Christian Medical Ministry is **to build committed multipliers...in the context of a movement...to influence and impact the medical community in order to send them to the world.** How can this vision be fulfilled? **THINK BIG!** When I look through Jesus' eyes upon my circumstances, I don't consider the size of a Goliath; instead, I thrill at the bigness of Jesus and ascribe power to Him only. A slingshot and five smooth stones take on tremendous proportions when I see His plans and purposes. Our hearts yearn to make an impact.

The story is told of Napoleon's soldiers carrying a map of the world over their hearts. Why? So, they wouldn't be thinking of the mud, the shortage of food, and tired bodies. Daily this military leader wanted his men to think in terms of world conquest. You should be carrying this vision...in your heart.

Pray that God will give you eyes that see...with an unconquerable optimism in contrast to a defeated pessimism. The individual of vision is always the individual of adventure. **The fruit is out on the limb... climb out on the limb and watch God take care of you.**

THINK BIG!

—•••—

A SHRIEK OR A PRAYER?

There are five levels of communication. **Level I–Cliché**, verbal garbage that are casual statements such as "How are you?" "Fine. How are you?" **Level II–Fact**, with no personal involvement…no risk. **Level III–Ideas / Opinions**; this is when risk begins. You may say to a friend, "I think you should…" **Level IV–Feelings**; in this level, transparency and vulnerability begin to open up. **Level V–Total Honesty**; this is when you are honest with your emotions and you are open to the ultimate rejection.

What level of communication did your family use when you were a child? On what level do you and your spouse communicate now? What level of communication do you have with God? Do you just occasionally check in with God and say, "How are you? I'm fine." **Would you be willing to communicate with God on Level IV and Level V, sharing with Him your emotions?** Would you lavish upon Him the overflow of a heart filled with love? Would you risk communicating your anger to Him?

In the Lament Psalm 142, David shows us that successful prayer is expressed in four things: 1.) sincerity + intensity + specific address (verses 1 & 2), 2.) a manifest sense of helplessness, 3.) an unqualified dependence on God expressed by His confession of trust and petition, and lastly, 4.) a vow of praise (verse 7).

Can't you imagine how David felt. He is presently in the cave of Abdulum as indicated in I Samuel 22. There is no one there. He is lonely. He is in isolation. As he reflects, it was God who said that he was going to be the anointed King of Israel! So…what is he doing out in enemy territory being chased by Saul the present King, whom he had served by slaying Goliath? Now, of all things, the cave is in the territory of Goliath. As David reflects, he opens with a "**shriek**" when he cries out loudly. He does so with sincere intensity; in verse 1 he tells of his distress, verse 2 of his desires.

"We may complain 'to' God, but not 'of' God."

Saul was seeking David's soul, and David's soul was seeking God. What a haven! In his opening complaint, crying aloud, he expresses his anger, his deep-felt emotions, his loneliness. What cave are you in? Is your spouse not a Christian, not treating you the way that you want to be treated? Do people not communicate, or maybe they try to communicate too much? Is your rotation hard? Your partner a complication? The future looks fearful? You saw fifty patients today; fifty percent of them were on Medicare. Your son is drinking…too heavily. Your financial advisor just told you that the stock you invested in is going down and recommends you take a loss.

Would you be willing to communicate with God on the deepest level—open to rejection? David did. Look at Psalm 142 again. After a sincere intensity of address to God, David has a manifest sense of helplessness when he says, "**I** am hurting. **You** don't care. **They**, the enemy, are winning." But keep on reading for you will find he moves from his complaint. . . to a profession of trust (5). He expresses ongoing dependence as he says, "Only God is my refuge." Look at the words "Give heed to me, deliver me, bring me out of prison, out of this situation" (6). Lastly, he ends with a vow of praise (7).

> **"Prayer is the footage of life; praise is the flower."**

David's prayer was not a cold and formal petition. It was aglow with intense and deliberate asking. When the warmth of earnest feeling and the holy art of definite pleading are present. . . it is surely effectual prayer.

Anointed prayer will have the element of desperate need. It is not the arithmetic of prayers...how many they are. It is not the rhetoric of our prayers...how eloquent they are. It is not the geometry of our prayers...how long they are. Prayers are answered when an urgent need is perceived with an earnest desire to have that need met.

> **"We often pray so little because we feel so little."**

Just as your spouse desires honest communication with you, and you with him or her, so God desires honest communication with you.

> **Be honest with God. He already knows. He has been honest with you. He desires that you communicate with Him at Level V.**

•••

ABC

Being with ER physicians, I often pondered, "How do you know what to do first?" The reply is, "You use the A-B-C-D and Es." For many years in the medical world the mantra of cardiopulmonary resuscitation (CPR) for someone who was in cardiac distress was defined by the ABCs. You start with making sure there is a clear airway; if the person wasn't breathing then a rescuer would have to do it for the victim with rescue breathing, and finally circulation must be continued if the heart wasn't beating with chest compressions. Over the years the system has changed to CAB, but that isn't in this study.

The Christian life is very much like the ABCs of CPR.

Airway

In order for a person to be resuscitated, he must have a means of getting oxygen into the bloodstream from an alternative source. If he can not get oxygen into the blood, he will die. The person without Christ is like a person who does not have a means of getting oxygen into the blood. The first thing that must be done is to establish an airway. In spiritual terms this is comparable to a person receiving Christ as his/her personal Savior and Lord. Until this is done, nothing else can be done for the "patient." His heart can continue to pump blood around his body, but if there isn't a source of oxygen and no way to get it into the blood, then the brain will not receive oxygen and he will die.

An oxygen debt will develop, and that debt must be paid in order for the patient to live. The oxygen that must be supplied can be compared to the atoning sacrifice that gives life through Christ. His work on the cross paid the penalty for our sins.

Breathing

Once the airway has been established, then oxygen must be supplied. If there is no source of oxygen and the patient is not breathing, then he will not get oxygen into the blood. So a source of oxygen must be present. Spiritually this is the same as God providing that oxygen source (atoning sacrifice of Jesus). Sometimes a patient has to be ventilated. Someone or something else have to help breathe.

People without God are unable to breathe. Therefore, God must breathe life into them spiritually. What is the role of the patient in all of this? Nothing! He can do nothing except let the doctors take care of him. If he is unconscious (spiritually dead), then he can do nothing to save himself. Someone else has to do it; that person is God.

Circulation

The third essential of resuscitation is circulation. Circulation is critical because it pushes blood to all the vital organs and delivers life-giving oxygen, plus it eliminates and filters out life-threatening toxins in the organs and bloodstream. The heart must function correctly in order to pump this life-giving blood rich with oxygen to the cells all over the body. In a resuscitation situation the heart is essentially dead. Without Christ our hearts are spiritually dead as well. However, God gives us a new heart and a new spirit (Ezekiel 36:26) when He performs his CPR on us.

Therefore, accepting Christ is like allowing God to perform CPR on us. He provides the oxygen (work of Christ on the cross that we couldn't do) and blood (sacrifice of God that we couldn't pay), and He cleanses and gives us a new heart and spirit (regeneration that we couldn't give).

Disability

Once we are resuscitated (saved), then God progresses to the next step of assessing our disability. We are alive, but the quality of our life may not be the best. So, this must be dealt with. God begins to assess our neurologic/psych status and works on it so that we can have a meaningful life. A person can be "saved" from death but be on a ventilator and not be of much use. He is alive, but he is unable to interact meaningfully with his environment. So, God begins to improve our "neurologic status" so that we can interact with others and carry out His plan for our lives. The purpose in saving someone is not just to save them to be a vegetable but to save them in order that they might be returned to a purposeful life.

Exposure/Environment

The next thing that is of concern is to expose the patient to make sure that there is not something else going on that would cause the patient to die (e.g., internal bleeding from broken bones, abdominal trauma, etc.). Every area of a person's life must be exposed and inspected to make sure that something is not overlooked…that some sin is not draining away the life God has given.

The patient must also be monitored for his temperature. His body temperature must be maintained. The environment his body is in must be kept warm. Spiritually this means seeking out a warm environment in fellowship with other believers. Unless this is done, a patient will become hypothermic and the new Christian's life will grow cold. He will be isolated and will not be aware of the falling temperature of his spiritual life.

Even in perfect conditions CPR works in only 18% of the times it is used. When God is involved, His CPR is always 100%. It is as easy as A-B-C.

—•••—

REMEMBER

"And you shall remember all the ways which the Lord your God has led you…that He might humble you, test you, to know what is in your heart." Deuteronomy 8:2

"Remember!" Twenty times in Deuteronomy this favorite counsel is given to remind us "not to forget." It has been said "for a person to sit down, and look back at their own attainments and personal doings, is about as wretched an occupation as anyone could engage in; it only brings barrenness, discouragement, and frustration." So, what do we remember?

Forget what you have done…never forget what God has done! Remember all His ways, not your own. Our past is loaded with labor and superficial efforts…His ways are loaded with comfort, corrections, training, and a multitude of those humblings and testings.

Talk about it…think about it…praise the Lord for it. As you look down the road ahead do it in the light of where you have been, but don't keep your eyes on the rear-view mirror of life.

CMMA started many years ago on June 1st. As we look at the past years, we see numberless interventions by God in our ministry. We could have done too much too soon. I remember how God's hand directed us at a certain divide in the road. One of the first board members wisely said among the rush of enthusiastic projects and events I was proposing at the end of one board meeting, "Let's do a few things well."

A look back over the shoulder assures you that He has led…and He is still leading today…and without question, He will lead in the days ahead!

A greater danger than adversity is affluence. Most people do not lose their faith when troubles come rolling in. However, it is easy to forget lessons learned about who is at the throttle of life when affluence comes tumbling in. Several verses in Deuteronomy show fixed foundations for our future. Don't try to hack it alone but "remember all the ways which the Lord your…

"God led you" (verse 2). We need a sense of God's presence.

"He fed you with manna." We need His daily provision.

"God is bringing you in" (verse 7). We need His guidance.

Trace God's gracious dealings in your life, and look for His tender guidance, His rich mercy, and the amazing fact of God's wondrous love, after our failures and sins.

Isn't it amazing to know that we are totally known by God and yet unconditionally accepted?

Paul says in Philippians, "Forgetting that which is past and stretching to that which is forward, I press on to the mark of the high calling which is in Christ Jesus our Lord." This day…this month…this year "press on daily," praying that many will see the beauty of our Lord Jesus Christ and respond in light of present realities, remembering what He has done for us.

—•••—

THE INTER.NET

The "Net" (pornography) is catching those who are casting their nets among fish that will kill your soul, your spirit, your spouse, and your children. Why? What need is met? Some men tell me they are angry. At whom?

According to Hebrew TALMUD, there are three ways of knowing a person: **"in their cups, with their money, and in their wrath."** Ill behavior at mealtime discloses bad upbringing. Bad conduct in business and finances discloses the unscrupulous. Ill-speaking in anger proclaims an unbridled spirit.

Proverbs helps us to know people **"in their cups, with their money, and in their wrath"** through four kinds of people: the Simple, the Wise, the Fool, and the Mocker (the Wicked).

> *"His own iniquities will ensnare the wicked, and he will be held with the cords of his sin."* Proverbs 5:22

Self-effort can never do the job of releasing a person who is caught in this net of his own making. The rebellious life is held prisoner by unyielding ropes. Habits grip. Evil deeds become evil habits. Do it once and it's a whole lot easier to do it again. Have you ever said, "I'll only do this once"? Now, you are imprisoned in a firm clutch where the power to resist is depleted. Our impulses increase as your motives decrease. You are a person so wrapped in the **"net"** of evil deeds that you commit the sin once more—not because you find any pleasure in it but for no better reason than you have committed it so often.

The habit becomes your master.

Note that "iniquities" of an individual "ensnare" them. As a person throws a **"net,"** whereby they catch the fish so the sins of a man become the means of catching the sinner. Like an octopus, "the ropes of a man's own sin drag him down and down and down. The lasso of lust and loose ethics incapacitate and deaden his testimony."

"You will be held by the 'cords' of your sin." At first, this evil inclination is like a spiderweb, but it finally grows into something like ropes of a ship. If not checked in the beginning, it becomes a root of habit that feels almost unbreakable.

You sow a thought…you reap an act.

You sow an act…you reap a character.

You sow a character…you reap a habit.

You sow a habit…you reap a destiny.

Samson's chains were at first made of mere grass and silk, and then were formed of iron and steel. It was on the lap of Delilah that the threads of the cable were being woven day by day until they could not be broken. Saul died on the battlefield by his own sword. Esau was caught in the cords of fleshly desires.

Can those cords be loosened and shattered? Take heart—the Cross of Christ has cut the cords of sin! When Jesus died on the cross, He died once for "All." Dr. Harvey Elder, infectious disease physician at Loma Linda University, said at a Medical Strategic Network Conference, "What part of **'ALL'** do you not understand?"

"He breaks the power of cancelled sin; He sets the prisoner free; His blood can make the foulest clean; His blood availed for me."

Stop casting the "net.".

———•••———

WORDS HEAL, NOT HURT

The quality of our words matches the condition of our heart. Christian love will change the Christian language as evidence in Ephesians 4:29, 32

> *"Let no unwholesome word proceed from your mouth, but only such a word as is 1.) good for edification, 2.) according to the need of the moment, and 3.) gives grace to those who hear…be kind to one another."*

An unkind Christian is a contradiction!

The word "be kind" is "chrestos," which means good, pleasant things, a kind person, useful, beneficial, and goodness in action.

Kindness is the fabric of a sincere Christian with an attitude of love toward others. If long suffering is love in the passive, then kindness is love in the active voice. Kindness is goodness in action expressing itself in deeds for others. Kindness is also likened to "wearing a smile" in the warmth of a Father's embrace.

In biblical times, if a poor man had no coals for a fire in cold weather, he would go out into the streets to beg. He would carry a pail on his head to let his needs be known. As he passed by the house of one with whom he'd been in conflict, and that person was Christian, there was only one thing to do.

The Christian would take "live coals" from his own fire and drop them out of his window into the beggar's pail. Thus, he would "heap coals of fire on his head" and make himself a friend for life **by this ungrudged kindness.**

"The fruit of the Spirit is love that issues in kindness."

Recognize your opportunity to relieve the sick, comfort someone in sorrow, help shoulder the load of someone staggering. You can do so much by your words, full of kindness and quietness in speech.

"Kindness is not an expression of weakness but the demonstration of the gentleness of strength."

Tender hearts produce words that heal. The opposite is a callused heart that tears down and holds hostage through moodiness, guilt trips, or psychological sabotage. (As a Phlegmatic, I do this with Judy!) Tough men are just often angry men. Words can hurt or they can heal. Unkind words put God through Gethsemane all over again. It breaks His heart, as well as discourages those whom He has loved.

Be imitators of God, as His Beloved children, and not only walk in love just as Christ walked in love but **become a wellspring from which healing words flows...**

———•••———

THE CUP

Have you been trying to understand, explain, answer what it means to "suffer" in this life? Or have you thought, as Paul seemed to embrace,

"I want to know Christ and the fellowship of His sufferings."
Philippians 3:10

Don Tabb, the pastor of The Chapel on the campus at Baton Rouge, used to say fellowship is "Two fellows on a ship going in the same direction." The Greek word Koinonia means to "hold in common." The Hebrews, when they celebrated Passover, had three cups. **"The Cup"** that Jesus used the night before His death was the cup of sin. All of our sins were poured into **"the Cup."** Christ, when He was crucified, drank **"the Cup"** on our behalf. Substitution!

Too often we think sin attracts us but does not blister us, interests us but does not burn us. We think we can gaze upon it with curious observation and it might not appear to create an emotional convulsion. We could see it laugh, we could see it sleep, but Jesus saw sin and wept. When a piano is out of tune to the refined ear it is disturbing. So, to an immeasurably deeper degree, should be the loss of companionship with Christ when we sin. It hurts.

Recently, there have been severe illnesses of doctors and fractured marriages—a time full of sorrow for the children especially. I've often thought, "I've got enough of my own!" When we add the fire of another person's suffering to our own, it is like the time when the Son of Man showed up in the furnace with Daniel's three friends. They were in the furnace but they were not burned, or hurt, or even had the smell of fire! When you feel the sorrow of another's sorrow, you are drinking "the Cup" of the Lord. You are saturated with the fellowship of His sufferings.

Our Lord served other people to the point of physical weakness, exhaustion, and eventually death. Our service too frequently ends where the bloodletting begins. Yet, it is just at that point of resistance that we begin to win.

"You have not yet resisted the point of shedding your blood."
Hebrews 12:4

When you serve others, it becomes costly. Example, Mother Theresa. What was her attraction? Her life became contagious when it became sacrificial. If you grab the goblet of suffering, say, "If it is possible, may 'this Cup' be taken from me, yet not as I will but as You will" (Matthew 26:39).

I feel the sorrow of so many. But looking back on the years since 1968 when Judy and I took off from Birmingham to join Campus Crusade for Christ with great joy, we had hearts desiring to reach the world for Christ. Now as I see my sun is setting, Son rays reflecting on the water of life, I know the joy of drinking **"the Cup"** of sacrifice and service, producing a clear, emotional, firsthand grasp on **"knowing Him, and the fellowship of His sufferings."**

——•••——

I'LL NEVER HAVE THE LOVE I WANT

Have you ever said…

"I'll never have the love I want"?

Due to the childhood incidents of binges with alcoholism of my father, it became lodged in me…Earle, you are on your own!

To control this, I made a 'vow' in my heart:

I won't need anyone…Not deeply…I can make it…without love.

But as I got older, my heart refused to live in my self-created isolation. I looked for someone to fill the void in my life, left by my father.

I chose Judy to be the lucky girl!

Since I perceived no one had ever really loved me, the way I so desperately thirsted to be loved, I gave her the chance. It lay in Judy's powers to validate my soul!

This pressure is more than any human being can bear. She, as we all do, had her own needs. Are you doing this? Satan closed in like a shark smelling blood, suggesting,

"Don't accept her love…it's not enough."

So I turned to my "false" love, losing myself in ministry like many in Medicine (that looked good!), escaping by trying to escape. I tried, even having trusted Christ at age 29, to love beyond my "longing to be loved"…but it eluded me.

Several years ago at a Board Retreat at Lake Martin, I heard Brennan Manning so penetratingly say, "God loved me in the sunshine and shadows, in the morning sun and evening rain. God can not stop loving me." I cried, "But isn't that too good to be true?" I still felt… alone!

I go to bed late, get up early, and in the wee hours of the morning, I hear my honest thoughts from the depth of my soul:

"I'll never have the love I want."

How long would this aching jump into my lap? Grabbing a Bible, I read:

"And as He has loved those who were His own in the world…HE LOVED THEM TILL…THE END." John 13:1

To the End! To the End!

This brought more hope than I have ever known, causing me to embrace my longing to be loved and turning the validation of my soul's needs over to my Father, my Abba. Jesus did come "to heal the broken heart."

Job exposed the ruling sentence of his heart: "What I feared has come upon me." Satan said, "You can't trust God with the things that mattered the most." Job's idol was "control." However, God was determined to save him from it. If you stay in despair, in control, you stop your heart from being captured by the ravished, reckless love of God.

The issue: Will I trust the great heart of the Father or shrink back in faithless fear? Will I trust God's heart, even if I can't see His hand?

Even though I don't remember many touches as a child, now I must risk Abba's touch (to cause or permit a part of the body to come in contact with, so as to feel). Touch kindles desire…desire is kept alive by imagination, the antidote to resignation. You cannot out-dream God. Faith draws courage. Things will change. There is hope. Our Beloved is on the path with me!

Have you ever said **"I'll never have the love I want"**?

Will you believe a lie…

"Let God be true and every man a liar." Romans 3:4

or…the truth?

"That the world may know that Thou has loved them even as Thou has loved me." John 17:23

Meditate…Drink deeply…Release…the reckless love of Jesus.

———•••———

SPIN DOCTORS

Do you see the life of Christ being hassled, hurried, or hurting people to fulfill His objective? Why not? Because He only did what He saw His Father doing.

> *"My Father is working unto now and I myself am working...Truly, truly I say unto you the Son can do nothing of himself unless it is something he sees the Father doing. For whatever the Father does these things the Son also does in like manner."* John 5:17, 19

We can't see God working in us because we are so busy spinning in the centrifuge of our life that is pushing us all to the outer limits.

My observation is some doctors are often so busily focused on the **"having"** (our possessions) and the **"doing"** (our work). Either we possess our possessions or they will possess us. Things do break down!

"You have to manage your 'stuff'...if you have 'stuff.' "
—Dr. Jim Strickland, Critical Care Specialist, Kirklin Clinic

Moving into the circle we see our **"doing,"** which consists of busy patient schedules, calls, conferences, CME, and other wonderful activities that generate enough income to obtain the **"having."** It can take away from the rest of the circles of **"relating,"** to our family, or our **"being,"** which is taking care of our own self, and lastly our **"primary loyalty"** of investing time without relationship with Jesus.

How did Christ handle the **"having"**? He had no place to lay His head; he admonished the disciples in Matthew 6 not to worry about how they would eat or drink or how they were clothed because the Heavenly Father knows the need of these things. Jesus said, "Seek first His Kingdom and His Righteousness and God will provide all of your needs." **Doing,** Jesus did what He saw the Father do. If we were so in touch with God and we did only what He asked us to do, it would take away some of the hassles of our life such as the "if onlys" and the "oughts" and the "I should do more of"...perfectionism.

Jesus related at times to His family in an unusual way when he says...

> *"Who are my brothers and sisters? Those who do the will of My Father."*

But notice how he **related** to the woman caught in adultery in John 8.

"Neither do I condemn you, go and sin no more."

He is saying, "You are such a wonderful lady. I am grieved that you have been used and abused by these religious leaders. For you to have sexual intercourse apart from the marital bond is only to hurt yourself. Please, don't do that anymore. I don't condemn you." (And He does the same for you and me.)

Jesus **"being"** is seen by His early morning prayers to the Father to see what the Father is doing and what His will is. Jesus' **"being"** was not just spiritual, in terms of prayer, but we find him in a boat going to the other side after a long day of teaching, and His **"being"** was asleep in the midst of a great storm.

His **"primary loyalty"** was shown in His statement of John 14:30 of how He loves the Father and how much the Father loves Him. At His baptism God said,

> *"This is my…beloved…Son of whom I am well pleased."*

What is His answer to being a Spin Doctor? Is it to just stop "doing" and "having" so we can "relate" and "be" a person and develop our "primary loyalty"? Not many I know in the medical profession would buy that. I think the answer is like a ballerina performing ballet when she spins with great beauty. She maintains her balance by focusing on a fixed point. The answer is for us to focus on a fixed point…the primary loyalty of the center circle out of which will allow us to maintain our balance…while we spin the days of our lives.

How is your **"doing"** and **"having"**? Won't you join with me…by focusing on our **"primary loyalty,"** the fixed point of Jesus?

LOVABLE

When we are loved and valued for our contributions, we have the ability to

… decrease fear

…build confidence

…and encourage compassion.

If we are perceived "lovable," we make it easier for others to love us. Our love also becomes an instrument to enable other folks to be lovable. I am talking about loving the other when there may not seem much to love—lots of giving and not much receiving. **Hearts follow value.** Take care of what you value, for if you love it, you will nurture it. Having given so much pre-marriage counseling and officiated many weddings, I see the courtship/romance phase and then the settling down phase when realities of life have broken in.

There is no denying that the unresponsive, unloving object of our love often becomes a bur under our saddle blanket.

> "The proof of love is its capacity to suffer for the…
> object of its affection."

"Lovable" people act in loving ways not because they always feel like it or perceive the value of the object loved; they do it because they feel they are loved by Jesus. The overflow of God's grace and love holds relationships together in these days of wash-and-wear wedding dresses. We live in the midst of people who are long on romance and short on the waterfall of God's love!

You mean I am stuck with her? That is exactly what I mean.

An elderly lady in South Alabama was busy kneading a batch of bread dough. Noting that her old woodstove needed replenishing, she pulled her hands from the dough and scurried to the woodpile to split an armload of firewood. Returning to the kitchen, she reloaded the stove. Her teenage granddaughter turned to her and said, "Grandma, how long does a honeymoon last?" "Till there is dough on the ax handle, Honey…till there is dough!"

Love is often perceived to be a sun-splashed, honeymoon-flavored emotion fueled by romantic nonsense of every sort. But let the dough get on the ax handle and then marital compatibility becomes for many the impossible dream.

Marital compatibility? That is a myth. Because of the selfishness of people, marriage duets often become duels. Marriage is the process of living with incompatibilities. Two selfish people learn how to live together. Love is the supernatural motivating force and the set of behaviors that pursue the resolution of these incompatibilities. Lovable folks carry WD40 not sandpaper. A marriage license is just a learner's permit!

Be honest with yourself. The people you really love are those who love you. When you perceive such as close friends, sweethearts, or lovers, love has reached that highest level of friendship, warmth, and intimacy.

"Hope...does not disappoint because...the love of God has been poured out within our hearts through the Holy Spirit who is given to us."
Romans 5:5

Would you be willing to treat yourself the way Jesus loves you?

———•••———

COMFORT IN THE SEASONS

God is the God of all comfort. **ALL COMFORT**

> ...No Limitations
>> ...No End
>>> ...No Circumstance or Person Excluded

If you are an uncomfortable Christian, then the only thing to give you a thoroughly comfortable religious life is to know who God is.

What do we know?

We know (1) God has revealed himself. He has not stuttered! (2) We must accept this revelation by believing what He has chosen to reveal. Although Christians profess to be followers of "the God of all comfort," often we spread gloom and discomfort around. Our sorrowful looks and dejected tones of voice show our hearts. If we're under the pile, the question is: "What are you doing there?"

We are to be "living epistles," known and read by all men. What are people reading about us? People must read in our lives what they hear in our words or our lives are worse than useless. What are people reading? As Brennan Manning said, "Earle, if you're in love with Jesus, tell your face!" (Pray I will smile more!)

But you don't understand... How can I be comforted when I have so much stress going on? It's in those moments that we receive comfort, pure and simply for what it is. God is like a mother who comforts her children. I've observed so many young couples by praying with them in the labor and delivery room and then seeing them at the Bible studies we held on Monday nights. As the child cried in the middle of our study, the mother comforted her child at the breast, or by her touch...her look...her voice.

As you're crying out now with salary cuts, personnel conflicts, insurance discord, and destructions, will you allow God to be your **"God of all comfort"?**

The seasons vary each year. We're leaving blue skies, soft warm breezes, scented flowers, and green grass to receive fall storms that baffle and barren winters that leave one stripped and cold.

When you feel this, it isn't that God has forsaken; it's just that law of spiritual seasons. Winters are not something to be endured, as in "I'll just put up with it until spring comes." Behind the storms of suffering, guilt, fear, anxiety, depression, or even indifference, there is the sufficiency of God for that day's crisis.

When I was in the lumber industry, I observed that the trees that were the strongest were those that had the most annular rings. These rings are formed in the winter, as compression collapses cells. While the tree doesn't appear to be fruitful, it is the most fruitful period of time! Those annual rings are for when storms come; it allows the tree to do what it was designed to do. Even architects have realized that with buildings, they are to bend and not break.

Are you in the season of life when the trees of your life are leafless, you feel the ground is frozen, and the wheat fields are brown and desolate and all you know to do is live by faith? **God...is...at...work!**

Job knew that the winter was to be followed by spring; darkness was only the prelude to light; pruning would make possible more fruitage; out of death comes new life. Are you discovering what Job did?

> *"For He directs the snow, the showers, the storm to fall upon the earth. Man's work stops at such time, so that all men everywhere may recognize His power."* Job 37:6

Jesus is the God of all comfort. Will you join me as I crawl in His lap, lay my head on His breast, hear the heartbeat...and be comforted beyond measure. What a mystery!

—•••—

BANKRUPTCY

Countless Christians today are in the midst of utter failure…that they know. What they do not yet know is that they are in the midst of their Father's purpose for them.

"Failure does not have to be final, but can be fruitful."

People, circumstances, and things are never the cause of failure. Self's reaction to them is the cause and the one problem to be dealt with. Failure is all part of God's plan to teach the believer total reliance on Him and total mistrust of self.

"He must increase, but I must decrease." John 3:3

Many children of God today have all but given up. Self and the world's system have been steadily taking over in their once bright Christian lives and service. Most have simply quit trying to live the Christian life: Many have become sick and tired of church for various reasons and no longer attend. They seek to carry on, trying one thing after another, but never find His answer to the hunger and need of their hearts. They think the only alternative is to quit as gracefully as possible…and get into something that they can handle.

"God is working for something beyond the immediate; He is working towards His glory."
—H. Foster

God undertakes our training with the intention that however difficult in practice the course may be, it will yield the "peaceable fruit of righteousness" in the lives of those who undergo it.

This represents His norm—no shortcuts and no exceptions. Think of Abraham, Joseph, Moses, or any others in the eleventh chapter of Hebrews. Their training lasted for decades and led them into painful situations…in difficult places. Their lives, as a result, were incomparably fruitful.

God allows us to experience failure as a result of self-effort in the Christian life. Often, we feel our failure proves that God cannot make use of us. In reality He is bringing us to the place where He can begin to use us!

He is not looking at us reproachfully because we cannot do the things that please Him. He knew all along that we cannot, and **He is watching over us in unchanging**

love… waiting until we learn the lesson that is necessary.

These are the very conditions the Father uses to prepare us to enter into that which He has already given in the Lord Jesus. The answer is to go from believing "on" Him at Calvary to living "in" Him in heaven. We go from substitutionary atonement to a personal identification. As defeated believers, we have to be prepared by the Spirit in order to abide in the Lord Jesus…as our life.

Isn't it first *"O wretched man that I am, who should deliver me from the body of death" and then "I thank God through Christ Jesus our Lord"* (Romans 7:24-25)?

"Progress involves risk; you cannot steal second with your foot on first."

If there is bankruptcy of self, you have riches in Christ. **Remember that through all of your failure, your Father is working…for your victory** (Proverbs 27:6).

—•••—

RESULTS?

Would you agree with this premise? Results in themselves are not proof that God is pleased. Results seem to be the "bottom line" whether it's ministry or medicine. It is easy to be captivated by the measuring stick of results to determine success.

Moses faced this. Moses had attempted great things for God by getting the Israelites out of Egypt. Don't you like Moses' brazen perspective of wanting to see the face of God? Moses and God were close. They were friends.

However, when the nation of Israel was in a no-water situation, they assembled themselves against Moses and Aaron. The people of Israel were blaming Moses for bringing them into the wilderness to die. They spiritualized their pagan life back in Egypt in contrast to the wretched place they were in. What would you have done? Moses came to the presence of the Lord, fell on his face, and when the Glory of the Lord appeared to him, the Lord told Moses to "take the rod along with Aaron, his brother, assemble the congregation, and speak to the rock before their eyes that it may yield its water. You shall thus bring forth water for them out of the rock and let the congregation be strengthened" (Numbers 20:8).

Good, so far, but verse 9 says, "Moses took the rod from before the Lord just as He had commanded him and gathered the people and said to them, 'Listen now, you rebels, shall we bring forth water for you out of this rock?' (Numbers 20:10). Then Moses lifted up his hand and struck the rock twice with his rod and water came forth abundantly and the congregation and their beasts drank."

Moses got the Israelites out of Egypt. He was not able to get them into the Promised Land. Was Moses a success? No, for while his disobedience brought forth water, it also brought punishment since God kept him from going into the Promised Land with all Israel. God's work must be done in His way. . . for His credit.

In Luke 10:19-20 Jesus says in effect not to rejoice in successful service but rejoice because you are rightly related to Me. It is so easy to rejoice in the fact that God has used you. What if you do not perceive that you are being used? Could you rejoice? Well, you can never measure what God will do through you if you are not rightly related to Jesus Christ. In fact, it is His mercy that as He pours Living Water through you, He doesn't let you know it.

The tendency today is to put emphasis on service. Beware of making usefulness your ground of appeal. If you study the life of Jesus, there are things He did that do not appear to be useful. However, the Spirit of God was working through Him. No less is He doing that in and through you.

Isn't it comforting to know that you can have a vital relationship and watch Him produce **results?**

THREE FACES OF LOVE

Christians possess a wondrous power.

> **"Perfect Love casts out fear."** 1 John 4:18

Did you ever consider solving your problems with the overflowing, unconditional, unmerited **love of God?**

In personal relationships, instead of handling conflicts by arguments and quarrels, deal with them with **love.** Self-centeredness creates fear. Fear creates storms and strife.

But love stops fear! "Everyone that **loves** is born of God and knows God" (1 John 4:7). To **love** is really to demonstrate that we know God. What are the faces of **love?**

Phileo (Because of) is a brotherly love that **must be shared** with another. It must be reciprocated or it will die. **Phileo's** origin and strength is intellectual. It is propelled by mutual interest and shared secrets and, as C.S. Lewis said in **"The Four Loves,"** is pictured as two people standing side by side, looking at the world from the same unique view of reality, which they feel is their **Phileo.**

Eros (If) is composed of four ingredients: imagination, proximity, contact, and emotion. **Eros love** seldom ever sees love as she or he really is. **Eros** is so highly charged that it goes off like a rocket. **Eros** has a short life unless it's replenished with other types of love. C.S. Lewis described this as "two persons looking face to face, seeing only each other." The paradox of this is, in marriages, the closer we happen to be to each other, loving with **Eros** alone, the more likely we are to be discourteous to each other. Haven't you seen marriages killed by little discourtesies? Ammon said he loved his half-sister, Tamar; but after he consummated his physical passion, he said "the hatred with which [he] hated her was greater than the love with which [he] loved her." Haven't you seen this truth?

Agape (In spite of) love is unconditional…sacrificial—a love that is instituted by the volitional will of God. It is the love for the unlovely. C.S. Lewis called this "a gift love" since it flows out of the mind and attitude. Because Agape is a love brought forth by the will, it alone is capable of responding to God's commandments. That is, if we **agape** God, we will **love** our brothers.

You may be unsure or feel inadequate, depressed, or disillusioned. But you are not that. You are accepted. Never confuse your perception of yourself with the mystery that you really are accepted.

When we accept that Jesus accepts us, we decrease our hunger for power, acceptance, or demands to be popular because we are enfolded in the arms of our Abba's security. Rest, my child…Rest!

I have seen this love in the eyes of fathers in medical school at the birth of their child: "Looks like me! See that smile? What a mystery. Will you bless her?"

Your **agape** love of God reveals the proof of your regeneration. **Agape** cares. **Agape** is not an emotion; it's caring in action. At times I've felt like I've run out of gas when caring about people who don't care about themselves or even when they don't return the love. But that only shows that I'm not dipping into the well of "living water." The source of Jesus' love is never exhausted.

God will bring across your path those who will love you unconditionally and yet others who are the most obnoxious whom you are to love unconditionally.

"O teach me, Father, how to love the most
Those who stand in need of love…that host
Of people who are sick and poor and bad, Whose tired faces show their lives are sad,
You know us, God of grace and peace above,
My one desire now: teach me to love!"
—Anonymous

Be the receiver, be a giver, be the vehicle. Loving what God loves.

•••

TWO CHARCOAL FIRES AND A ROOSTER

Peter's denial was given in the light of a **charcoal fire.**

> **"And a certain servant girl seeing him as he sat in the fire light and looking intently at him said, 'This man was with Him too!' But, he denied it, saying, 'Woman, I did not know Him.' "** Luke 22:56-57

After the denial, the rooster crowed. Why does God send crowing roosters into our lives? Because He loves us. He cares enough to schedule corrective surgery knowing full well that you sometimes have to hurt before we can heal. God cares enough to communicate!

Love is a rooster that crows, shatters silence, rejects neutrality, challenges apathy, and affirms purity. A straightforward warning to Peter's ears seemed sealed by his own self-confidence when he said, "Even if all fall away on account of you, I never will." "Even if I have to die with you, I will never disown you" (Matthew 26:33, 35). You can count on me Lord. When the fires of temptation or trials are burning hot and the resolutions of good intentions are prone to go up in smoke, talk is cheap.

It is tough to stand alone, to be the odd man out, to resist rejection. Just as the Lord predicted, His flock fled when the crunch came. Peter followed from a distance, warming himself at the fire hoping to blend into the crowd. He didn't. The little servant girl blew his cover!

After the third denial, the rooster crowed. ***"The Lord turned and looked straight at Peter" (Luke 22:61)*. What a gaze that must have been!** Compassionate? Hurting? Questioning? Touching? The rooster's crow rings clear to those who are committed to growing in love…to maintaining purity of heart, integrity of conscience, and authenticity of life.

How should we respond when the rooster crows? Peter remembered the Word that Jesus had spoken. This was a call to the Truth.

"Maturity is always an appropriate response to Truth, even when it hurts."

It often does.

Peter slopped into the night. He wept bitterly. Tears fell down those dark cheeks. Peter sobbed. How could he have said that he didn't know Him? He reviewed all of the "If onlys." He sold out his heritage, his reputation, his best friend. Peter felt it was over; he was finished.

Not knowing what else to do, Peter goes back to the familiar…fishing. On the water he could try to forget the wounds of his failure. But, Jesus comes to restore Peter, making a **charcoal fire;** he lay fish on it and calls Peter to come fellowship with Him. Following their simple breakfast, Jesus turns to Peter and asks that probing question three times: **"Do you love me?"** Three times he had denied, and three times he affirms his love. Jesus asked, **"Peter, do you love me more than these?"** Remember the object of your affection—will you sacrifice this for me? Do we love Him more than our careers, our securities, or even our worldly treasures? When you boil it down, the issue is always love. We cannot serve two masters. Never could, never will.

Two people heard the rooster on that day. One resisted and died; the other repented and lived. Although Judas' suicide was relatively quick, he died inch by inch. Each time he heard the Master speak and was unresponsive; each time he experienced Christ's love and was unmoved; each time he witnessed the Lord's power and was indifferent… he died. He sowed an act and reaped a destiny.

Thank God for roosters! Immediately a rooster crowed and **Peter remembered The Word.** People who develop a habit of responding to God's words become Christ-flavored people. Lovable people. People who are truly alive, authentic, beautiful, sincere. When you fall, when you hear the rooster crow, come running back into the open arms of Jesus.

Two charcoal fires and a rooster. He will feed you…and free you…at the charcoal fire.

—•••—

OUTSIDE VOICE

What are you worth? Whoever owns something puts a price tag on it. Then, he writes out what it's worth. Have you written on your own price tag what you're worth? Adam was asked by God to name all the animals. Why? Adam, as he looked into a pool of water, saw his face reflected. He then realized in contrast to the animals that he **"needed a voice outside"** of himself to answer the question **"Who am I?"** What outside voice do we listen to?

Jesus was constantly listening to his Father. His Father said, "This is my Son, in whom I am well pleased." Jesus listened in prayer. Interestingly, John says the Word was made flesh. Hebrews says that Jesus was the Final Word. Think about it. God has spoken in His Son; He has not stuttered. God has said that since we are made in the image of God, we are of infinite value…unconditionally loved…limitless love. We were not God's last chance, but His first choice. When you were in grammar school and they were choosing sides, were you chosen first or last? If you were chosen last, as I was, how did that make you feel?

There are other voices that we can listen to—our family, friends, colleagues, patients, and particularly our spouses. Are you hearing what you want to hear from them? Stop and think for a minute; you'll probably find this is where you are having conflict. How dare they not tell me what I desperately need to hear!

Adam, in the garden, listened to God and knew **"who he was."** After the fall, which was precipitated by his listening to the voice of Satan, who said, "God is cheating you. If you will just be independent of God, you will be like God."

Adam made the choice and so have we, with the same results…to be our own god. We are even asking God to walk beside us, not be in control inside us. If we are a god, we are supposed to know the future, and I don't, so I feel shame. A god is supposed to be perfect, and I am not, so I feel guilt and shame.

Adam and Eve, after they listened to the wrong voice, did two things. When they became aware, they were naked and ashamed and they hid from God and hurled accusations at Him. Interestingly, we do the same thing in marriage: We hide from each other. Has your wife ever said to you, "Who are you? Let me know the insides of you. You just never share." We hurl accusations of anger at each other. All of this is a fig leaf approach to cover our inadequacies—and for only one reason: We have chosen to **believe the**

lie...rather than to believe the Truth.

> *"You are not your own. You have been bought with a price...with precious blood, as of a lamb unblemished and, the blood of Christ."*
> 1 Peter 1:19

Look at your price tag. Let God write on it. The One who created you cherishes you. He takes pleasure in you, and He longs for an intimate relationship with you because, having been created in His own image, you have infinite worth. Or, are you listening to all the other voices?

Assimilate Jesus' final words to the disciples in John 17. "The world will know that You sent Me and will understand that You love them as **much as** you love me." As much as! Amazing!

Will you listen? Will you hear the Truth? Or will you do as I have on different occasions and believe the lie? Oh, how it hurts me and hurts others who love me.

> *Don't you want your children to believe that you really love them rather than living the lie? Can you imagine what God feels? You are His child.* **Listen to His voice!**
> —Anonymous

Be the receiver, be a giver, be the vehicle. Loving what God loves.

CHAPTER TWO

WARFARE

—•••—

GETTING OUR ATTENTION

God often allows us to experience circumstances that will enable us to see how blindly we succumb to Satan's deceptions. What is an example of Satan's lie? **FEAR OF FAIL-URE.** So often "fear" is the driving force in the lives of the medical/dental profession-al—fear about getting in, staying in, or finding a practice. Fear drives us to perform. Sadly, our self-worth is then tied to that performance.

Life does present its daily "how come?" There are perplexities that cause a person's heart to pound and ties his or her stomach in knots. "Why, Lord...why?" bewilders and bogs us down. However, there is no night too dark for God or any knot too complicated for Him to untie.

> *"Don't doubt in the dark what God has shown to you in the light."* —Oswald Chambers

God is the perfect problem solver. He knows all the details behind every "how come?" Even in the pressure of circumstances, nothing touches our life that God Himself isn't speaking. Do we discern His voice? Every time circumstances press, say, "Speak, Lord." Make time to listen to Him.

Peter walked on water when he focused on Jesus. When he saw the wind...the circum-stances...he was afraid, and he sank. What was the difference? Not the circumstance but his focus caused him to go down. Rumors...questions...doubts are all rampant in the medical community. Does the future hold fearful changes...restrictions? What is going to be your focus?

How you weather the future storms will depend on your root system. Job shows that the real person is revealed as surface things are removed. Though disease was in Job's body, God was still in Job's heart. The howling wind of circumstantial tempta-tions will soon reveal if a person has a "cut flower" character...beautiful to look at, but no root. Shaking removes the artificial! God is in charge of circumstances. Look at what He changes:

> **"He changes rivers...into a wilderness, and springs of water...into a**
> **thirsty ground, and a fruitful land...into a salt waste, because of the**
> **wickedness of those who dwell in it. He changes a wilderness into a**
> **pool of water and a dry land into springs of water; and there He makes**
> **the hungry to dwell, so that they may establish an inhabited city,**

and sow field, and plant vineyards, and gather a fruitful harvest."
Psalm 107:33-37

The lessons of circumstances teach us that "success" or "failure" is not the basis of our self-worth. If we evaluate ourselves by performance, we are ultimately going to lose no matter how successful we are at the moment. False beliefs, resulting in painful emotions, affect our self-worth. Instead of trying to change situations, we need to change our false beliefs.

"Why do you let the troubles of tomorrow bring sorrow to your heart and burdens too? For…if your Father's eye is on the sparrow then…surely He will care for you. He knows…He cares…each burden…He bears, for if the Father's eye is on the sparrow then…surely He will care for you."

"With all my tribulation, I am filled with comfort; I am overflowing with joy." 2 Corinthians 7:4

Are your false beliefs affecting your feelings of self-worth? Have you been reacting to circumstances, or have you reasoned through to think and believe correctly? The solution?

Act on the Word of God.

———•••———

NEEDS

*"You will never know Jesus is ALL you **need** until Jesus is ALL that you have."*
—Corrie ten Boom

If God is real, then He is all we **need**…no matter the trial.

If He is really there and we are His children, then He is all we **need**…no matter the pain.

However, often we are so concerned about our **"needs"** that we don't see Him…as all we **need.**

Take, for example, when the multitudes followed Jesus. Late in the day they expressed to the disciples their hunger. Five thousand of them. Did Jesus meet their **need?**

Yes…but having fed them, He began to teach them,

> *"I am the Bread of Life…he who eats physical bread will die…but he who eats this Bread shall live forever."* John 6:48-58

What was the response? Many of His disciples withdrew and were not walking with Him anymore.

Disciples!

Not his enemies or relatives, but His disciples. They left Him. (Peter didn't!)

Why?

Because they saw that being a disciple was not merely obtaining free lunches or having their every need met. Discipleship is an intimate, vital, eternal spiritual relationship with the Living-Eternal God.

Discipleship is not a program, a temporal-material need-oriented relationship with this miracle worker…but a living communion with the Jesus-in-the-flesh Son of God.

Since Jesus is reality, then **He is all we need.**

In His own words,

> *"The Spirit gives life…the flesh profits nothing, the words I have spoken to you are…spirit…and life."* John 6:63

Satisfied…but still hungry? Jesus is all you need!

—•••—

WHOLEHEARTEDNESS

What do you desire?

> *"Whom have I in Heaven…but Thee and there is none (zero, nothing, nil) upon earth that I desire besides Thee."* Psalm 73:25

But Thee…Besides Thee…Nothing desired!

Paul said he had learned that whatever state he was in to be content. He had to learn it. He was not restful by nature; he found it difficult. However, remember he is the one who wrote from prison with a shackle on his wrist and a headsman's ax hanging by a thread over his neck. Paul sent word to the church at Philippi, which was bathed in sunshine, not for the purpose of getting help but of giving help. What was Paul's secret? It was Jesus Christ…desired…appropriated…**wholly followed**…enjoyed.

C.S. Lewis discovered what Paul had experienced:

> *"God whispers to us in our joy and shouts to us in our pain. Pain is God's megaphone to get our attention."*

Don't you find that pain comes when you are seeking something that may seem to be good but is not God's best? God has an intense desire to meet your desires. How your thoughts perceive your pain is going to make a difference in your accessing resources for inner contentment.

Great **thoughts** of God create a great heart for God. You can't have great thoughts of God and small thoughts of yourself any more than you can have great thoughts of yourself without having small thoughts of God.

Great thoughts of God…
> make a poor person rich
> a fearful person brave
> a timid person bold
> an addicted person free!

Six times this distinctive title, **"Wholly followed,"** is used concerning Caleb. Could this be the secret of a heart that never went stale? He poured all he had into his life. His faith was like a ship that kept its course whether the sea was rough or smooth.

"Crisis times do not create character in an individual…they simply test and reveal what is already there."

The majority saw the giants; Caleb and Joshua saw God. The other ten saw their own weakness. What Caleb inwardly believed, he outwardly acknowledged, regardless of the consequences. Is "managed care" your giant?

How is your heart? Is it a great heart? A great heart is a new heart that has been submitted "wholly" to God to be filled with all the fullness of God. Great hearts are thirsty hearts…hearts that refuse **trickles** and demand **torrents.**

> ***"If any man is thirsty [for a great heart],"*** *Jesus cried in a loud voice,* ***"let him come to Me and drink…and out of his innermost being shall flow rivers of living water."*** John 7:37

Your freedom lies in where you put your mind. The disciplines of solitude, silence, and fasting can be used for you to create a thirst and desire for the correct food. Are you eating God's food (for instance, John 6:63) or are you eating dog food? Sin is slop. Be as unwilling to take sin into your heart as you would be to take garbage into your mouth.

Change comes by engagement. You must act. To learn to swim you must jump in the water and take lessons. For some to be healed, Jesus asked them to stretch out their hands. **Will you stretch out your hands now? It is an act of faith so that God can give great things to those with great hearts...who have great thoughts of Him.**

What is it that you really desire? Be a Caleb, wholly (holy) follow Jesus.

—•••—

FEAR

Who knows? Buy-outs, buy-ins, join-ins, kicked out. . .Blue Cross cuts you 12% across the board. Uncertainties produce fear.

Fear makes our world smaller.

When fear attacks we pull back, retreating rather than meeting it head-on. We hide at home...sleep...overeat...make excuses to avoid the problem.

> *"All of us have reservoirs of full potential—vast areas of great satisfaction. But the road that leads to those reservoirs 'are guarded by the dragon of fear.' "*
> —Paul Tournier, *The Strong and the Weak*

Open Psalm 27 to see how David faced these violent storms of life. The outline is Warring (1-3), Worshipping (4-6), Walking (7-12), Waiting (13-14).

> ***"The Lord is my light and my salvation. Whom shall I fear? The Lord is the defense of my life; Whom shall I dread?"*** (v. 1)

When David talks about fear, the first Hebrew word means "anxiety and agitation." The second use is "Pachad," meaning "to be in awe or to be intimidated."

In the midst of darkness, the Lord is light. In the midst of death, He is a salvation. In the midst of the storm, David sees his God.

Beyond the clouds, the sun is always shining.

Where are you looking? Look up at a fixed point. God.

Salvation gives light to those who sit in the valley of the shadow of death. His light is within us, around us, and it is to be reflected through us. The uniqueness of light is that light was one of the first things that God made visible and created. The first thing we usually do is to turn on the light to do anything.

"Whom shall I fear?" This is a question which has its own answers. Light dispels darkness. When our children used to go to bed they would daily cry out that they wanted water and to turn on a small light. They really wanted our presence. If you have children now, time after time calling for water and light, please… please…go do it, for when they are grown, they don't call you anymore!

Are you faced with the burden of ill health…perfectionism…parents you don't measure up to…crippling anxieties? Have you experienced the treachery of a trusted friend…the load of financial pressure…reaction to your spouse…the tragedy of a child who sows to the wind who is soon to reap the whirlwind? Is there some sharp thorn of sorrow that you can not share with another living soul?

What must we do? We do what Psalm 55:22 says: **"Cast your burdens upon the Lord, and He will sustain you."** He has not promised to remove the burden, but He says He will sustain you. He says it isn't just that He carries the burden, but He also carries us. Crawl up in His lap. Rest.

The word "cares" originally signified the small branches of a tree. The arms of the tree shoot out in every direction, entangling and entwining themselves with one another. Let the wind take them…see how they feel. How restless and confused they become, striking one another. Man's mind is like that storm-beaten tree…thoughts and cares continually shifting…changing…beating.

What a mess! What are the possibilities for deliverance? **"Dwell in the secret place"…you do your part…He will do His. Aren't those great odds? Three to one.**

———•••———

SHINE

"And
I will lead the blind in a way they do not know,
I will guide them in paths they do not know
I will make darkness into light before them and rugged places
Into plains.
These are the things I will do,
And
I will not leave them undone."
Isaiah 42:16

I will lead, I will guide, I will make, I will not leave them undone. The almighty Elohim of Scripture is a God of purpose. Since we are created in His image, we also have the same volitional purpose of being free moral agents who do not have to choose, but can choose. Israel found this the case; between "coming out" of Egypt and the "going in" of Canaan lies a wilderness. What should have taken a couple of weeks became a forty-year breakdown. The children of Israel were trams and not travelers, wanderers but not pilgrims. They existed, but they were not living.

Is this true of you—a saved soul but a lost life? Are you on the treadmill of aimlessness? You are happy to have left Egypt, but you have not entered the enjoyment of Canaan? Bogged down in the desert, they spun their wheels around Kadesh of Barnea.

A Christian is always a loser if he fails to take advantage of the promises of God. When the stresses of life come, you will see the skeptic staggering and the man of God standing. One grasps at straws…the other one clings to the promises of God's Word. In the midnight of circumstances, most people fear the worst, but the Christian finds his or her faith feeding on the promises of God.

"Never doubt in the dark…what God has promised you in the light." —V.R. Edman

God has taken the darkness of an individual's life and flooded it with the light of the knowledge of God's glory in the face of Christ.

The Christian life is simple: "Walk in the light as He Himself is in the light." Then we have fellowship with one another.

Jesus knows your name, your family, your circumstances, your problems, your weaknesses, and your future. He has the answers for every one of your needs. The promises of God are free and unmerited if **we will** do three simple things:

Comply with the condition laid down.

Pray the promise into your life and then, by faith...

Believe God!

Together, let's cling and claim some promises of God.

"It has often been said the darker the day, the greater the light must shine."
—Leonard Ravenhill

You are light. . . so shine!

———•••———

BUT

Often, the most powerful, life-changing miracles seem to happen in the "buts" of life.

"When you are in the dark, listen, and God will give you a very precious message."
—Oswald Chambers

Consider Naaman (2 Kings 5:1)

...commander of the army of the King of Syria
...a great man with His Master
...a mighty man of valor.

Then out of nowhere...life-altering words:

BUT...he was a leper.

Leprosy—think about that:

...dreadful disease of his day

...putrefying infected sores

...loss of fingers, toes, nose

...outward, so others saw it and avoided him

...inward, it's a malady that defined who he was.

Christ followers understand this is their own journey.

You love God and believe God loves you

You read the Word, pray, give, Walk in the Spirit

BUT...
The doctor gives you terminal news.
BUT...
Your spouse left, and the hole in your heart grows deeper, wider.
BUT...
Your job was eliminated; you're in the unemployment line.
BUT...
Your son or daughter rejected your life-time nurture, and the relationship seems destroyed.

"Buts" now seem to define who you are. "Buts" lead to questions of God and His plan.

"Where are you, God?"

But...

A slave girl recommends Naaman travel to find Elisha (the prophet). Elisha sends a servant to instruct Naaman to go wash seven times in the Jordan. He rages how irrational the command is, and then he obeys.

How did Naaman feel after he dunks himself the first time?

No change.

The second time? No change.

The third time? No change.

After the sixth time, his anger increased, and he felt embarrassed.

THEN...Naaman dipped the seventh time and "his flesh was restored like the flesh of a little child...he was clean" (2 Kings 5:14). He went back to the man of God, stood, and declared,

> ***"Now...I know that there is no God in all the earth...but in Israel"***
> 2 Kings 5:15

God was in the midst of Naaman's pain:
...faithfully at work in the "buts" of his life,
....steadfast in His plan in Naaman's journey,
...which brought Glory to God.

Have you been there?

Faith…trust…obedience…and seemingly no change? Feeling confused, distraught, even angry with God.

God is in the midst of your pain:

…you are not forgotten or forsaken,

…He faithfully works his plan by taking your "story" and making it "His Story."

Don't give up! Just one more dip in the Jordan…might be the final "But"

Be Clean.

———•••———

THE GOD OF MONEY

Money can be a blessing or a burden. Think about how much news there is talking about the money we have and don't have, whether it is for wages, school, social security, business trouble. How much time and energy do you expend worrying over money? "It's not like when I started 20 years ago…"

People have ruined their health for it, shipwrecked their home, forfeited their integrity, and sacrificed their lives. Some people worship money and some deify it. Some beg, some borrow, and some steal it. Some inherit money; others merit it or marry it. The majority of us work for it. We all spend it. We all want more of it. I've never had enough! Is it true for you?

"The love of money is a root of all kinds of evil." 1 Timothy 6:10

Two things that our Lord centered His most scathing teachings on were money and marriage, because they are the two things that make men and women saints or devils. Covetousness is the root of all evil, whether it shows itself in money matters or marriage. The Compassionate Savior was hard-hitting on the proposition:

"You cannot serve both God and money." Matthew 6:24

The deceitfulness of what you own promises what it can never produce. Get wealth and then you will have prosperity, peace, and influence, one thinks. Solomon says, "It just isn't true!"

> *"To a man whom God has given riches, possession, and honor so that he lacks nothing for his soul of all that he might desire, yet God does not give him the power to enjoy, but gives to a stranger, this is vanity ...even though he lives a thousand years twice over, yet has seen no good or experienced no enjoyment, do not all go to one place. The place of death?"* Ecclesiastes 6:2, 6

"What can money do for you?" Its roads are full of mirages, enticing gleams of water, which vanish as soon as we draw near. One after another of the alluring pools turn out to be hot glowing sand piles. This condition, into which riches lead you, only intensifies your thirst.

You can't take riches with you, although Jesus said you could send it on ahead. Men attempt to lay up treasures for themselves by investing in stocks, 401Ks, and the like. Men lay up treasures for God by giving and sharing. The Holy Spirit teaches us to fasten our thinking upon God, since our real treasure is in heaven. God gives to some the honor of having riches, but he would give to all of us unconditional love, the wealth of a contented life. "Little is much with God in it." If you have riches, enjoy and share it.

> *"As for the rich in this present age, charge them not to be haughty, nor to set their hopes on the uncertainty of riches, but on God, who richly provides us with everything to enjoy. They are to do good, to be rich in good works, to be generous and ready to share, thus storing up treasure for themselves as a good foundation for the future, so that they may take hold of that which is truly life."* Timothy 6:17-19

Amazing! He actually says that whatever God has given, we are to enjoy! During Fall and Spring Retreats, where doctors let me use their lake homes for the medical school students, my enjoyment has been to share this privilege. Use money as the proper tool/stewardship, because...

"Any tool in the hand of a fool can be misused."

You cannot serve both God and money...The choice is yours.

———•••———

HOW COME?

"And he said, 'Naked I came from my mother's womb, and naked I shall return there. The Lord gave and the Lord has taken away. Blessed be the name of the Lord.' Through all this Job did not sin nor did he blame God." Job 1:21-22

Life has its daily: **"How come?"** Perplexities can cause a person's stomach to be tied up in knots and cause his or her heart to thump.

Job lost all but his life, only to gain from the hand of God twice as much. Job knew what it meant to be 'in hot water' but never forgot WHO had allowed it all to happen! No night is too dark for God, no knot too complicated for Him to untie, for He is the perfect problem solver. God knows all the details behind every **"How come?"**

These dilemmas of living completely bewilder and bog us down with the question **"Why, Lord…why?"**

Across my desk come many counseling opportunities with great needs and disappointments. Some come from marriages that are being fractured, others from disappointments of not receiving residencies that they earnestly desired on "match day."

Look at the life of Job. It shows that when you come to the end of your rope, tie a knot and hang on!

If we look to God for deliverance, we are prone to try to discover what material He has on hand to work with in coming to our relief. We look, and we crave for something in sight that will help the Lord out. We want to find a little something for God to begin on. Guess what? He doesn't need anything to begin on, for "in the beginning" God created the heavens and the earth out of nothing…absolutely nothing. The god that made Earth, sun, moon, and stars—can this God not supply all our needs? Even if we don't see He has anything with which to begin to work?

Can God? God can! Watch God operate through the darkest and most difficult circumstances. Making something out of nothing, bound only by the outstretched arms of Jesus…in the middle.

Tie a knot and hang on to the promises of God. The darker the night, the brighter are God's stars.

—•••—

CONFLICT AND CALM

A famous scientist is said to have thrown himself into a cab, calling out to the driver, "Drive fast." Away went the cab, jolting over the streets until he inquired: "Do you know where we are going?" The driver answered, "No…but I am driving fast!" **Isn't that the picture of the average practice?** More patients…more gold crowns…more procedures!

Jesus' life was lived in the loud, stunning tide of human care and communion. How did He do it? Can we?

He lived strenuously. Mark uses the word "immediately" to show the days were filled with swiftly moving succession of exacting tasks. Jesus' time was spent with multitudes…with individuals. Privacy was difficult to obtain.

Yet, Jesus was always serene. He never hurried. Even with the urgent message to come and save Lazarus, "He abode two days in the same place."

Interruptions never distracted Him. He accepted them as opportunities of a richer service. Those interruptions were the occasion of some of His most revealing words. **How do interruptions affect you?**

He lived intensely…yet without tension. Jesus was stirred to compassion so deep it affected Him physically as He saw the presence of human need. He was "grieved" at the hardness of men's hearts, He shed tears of sympathy as He stood with mourners, and He was broken with sorrow as He contemplated the judgment of desolation about to fall on Jerusalem. He reacted to hypocrisy, yet there was always the quick return to His calm dignity.

Jesus lived dangerously, yet always in the calm of invincible courage. His brothers said, "Don't go to Jerusalem," but He went anyway. He told the Pharisees that He had accepted His appointed course. Regardless of threats, He would fulfill it. When the soldiers arrested Him, they were awed by the majestic calm of Jesus. They shrank back in consternation, falling to the ground.

Jesus seemed to create a little island of quiet around Himself in the sea of excitement in which He moved. **How shall we account for this victorious calm?**

Consider His words: "Take my yoke upon you and learn from me, for I am gentle and humble in heart and you shall find rest for your souls."

Jesus says three things: (1) The way in which He adjusted to life made for ease and rest…"My yoke is easy, My burden is light"; (2) His yoke, or adjustment to life, was gentleness and humbleness; (3) Those who take His yoke upon them and learn of Him, are those who will meet life with a gentle and humble heart…**you will then find rest for your soul.**

> *"It is not your burden that weighs you down. It is your proud, rebellious self-seeking, self-pleasing heart…Had he dealt with you after your sins and rewarded you according to your iniquities, you would not have been here to find fault with the way He is leading you to pardon, peace, and everlasting light."* —Alexander Whyte

Self-centeredness makes of life…a field of tensions. The surrender of self is a very crucial, detailed, costly action, but nothing less will suffice. It will bring the happy result of a heart at leisure from itself with new possibilities of joyous living.

What cab are you jumping in, asking the cabbie to drive fast? Take Jesus' yoke and His burdens, for they are light; they are easy. **Watch Him supernaturally love with your heart…speak with your lips…touch with your hands…in conflict and calm.** ·

———•••———

LOVE OR PRIDE

"God, tell me you love me."
      "I love you…"
"Tell me again, God."
      "I love you…"
"I don't understand why? Why do you love me?"
"I can't stop loving you. Sometimes my passion is unreasonable…unfathomable… and unlimited.
      Rest, my child."

Love must be limitless; Christ knew Peter's faults. "Do you love me? Feed my sheep." Peter felt those faults very clearly. Yet, Jesus drew him back with "a saving look, a glance," as a mother does with a child she sees in danger through their own carelessness. Christ's love for Peter was boundless. "Peter is Peter, and I love him," Jesus says. He did not wait for him to become another man. Jesus' love enabled him to become the other man.

How do you love your spouse? Remember when you joyfully dated those who were opposite of you? After marriage, did you seek to change that individual to fit your own desires? Rejection, not acceptance, is set up, and thus begins the battleground. The motives are often good in that we wish it not merely for our own sake but for our spouse's benefit as well. Perfect love consists of being able to shower a person with love in spite of their weaknesses...faults...and imperfection. Give them the freedom to change, according to God's will!

The weaknesses of your lover do not necessarily make you a stranger to each other. It should make your relationship come closer, more intimate and inwardly together, in order to overcome the weakness. God has given you your spouse to complete and complement you, not compete with you.

It is important that we not imagine how we wish they "should be." He who allows himself to do this does not love the person he sees, but something unseen such as his own ideals. I did this recently with Judy.

Why? Missy, my daughter, was in the hospital in Vail with a collapsed lung. Judy was rightly feeling Missy's pain; I was the calm, cool professional reacting to the little things she needed me to do. Mark it down on your memory pad...whenever you are at odds with someone else, pride is heavily involved. Pride makes you impatient when someone contradicts your personal opinion, adds to your sentences, or tells you what you are about ready to say. Quarreling over rights and anything in the slightest could be proof positive you are downright...proud! Why is it so hard for us to say "I was wrong . . . forgive me"? Pride is hard to die!

"Love covers a multitude of sin."

Strive to protect the joy of loving the person you see. Love them...as you see them, with all their imperfections. Love them even though they no longer love you or have perhaps turned away to love another; love them when they betray you or deny you. Jesus did. Jesus will supernaturally enable you too!

"God, tell me..."
 "I did on the cross."

——•••——

STORMS

How do you handle the violent **"storms"** of life: physical ones…spiritual ones… personal ones?

> *"Though a mighty army surrounds me, my heart will know no fear, even if they attack me…I remain confident."* Psalm 27:3

David knew something of the trials and troubles through which we all pass.

Within our ministry, we recently cried over the death of a newborn, the rages of leukemia in a physician's sister who fought it for 9 months, and everything from staff conflicts within practices to malpractice suits. When you see the storms, do you have the attitude of David? "Whom shall I fear? Of whom shall I be afraid? I cry aloud with my voice…neither forsake me…deliver me or I will faint." In the midst of the "storm" he sees his God!

Beyond the clouds the sun is always shining!

How difficult it is to see God because of the magnitude of the storm! At times there is no place to look but up. Even as in Psalm 27:10, *"though your mother and father forsake or abandon you, but the Lord will pick you up into His arms."* Knowing God, you view your storm from a different perspective. Job's casual acquaintance with Yhwh left a lot of questions unanswered. His deep, abiding relationship. . . intimacy

…became supportive to life's problems.

What is the key? See verse 13.

> *"I am confident I will see the Lord's goodness*
> *while I am in the land of the living.*
> *Wait…for the Lord."*

This is a statement of faith. When you exercise faith, the clouds of despair rolling over your soul are blown away so you can see…the sun was always shining. When all of your tent stakes are knocked down, expect to see in the providence of God His goodness. You will be brought as a friend into the intimate room of who God is. Seeing God for who He is, you will never be the same. If you do not allow your children to risk, they will never know your strong arms. How do we expect God is going to reveal who He is except through the "storms" of life?

Paul, who had been beaten and battered, loved, depressed, downcast, elated, distressed, and joyful, basically said, "Nothing could ever separate us from the love of God, which is in Christ Jesus." 0 x 0 = 0. Nothing!

Whatever God loves, He loves without limit...caution...or regret...beyond measure...beyond worthiness and unworthiness...in the "storms"!

—•••—

WORRY

Worry...I am worried that I have worries! Have you ever felt that way?

Have you ever noticed what Jesus said would choke the Word? The devil? No, the cares of this world. It is the 'little' worries. I will not trust where I cannot see; that is where infidelity begins. The cure is a faith response to the revealed Spirit.

> *"He will guard him in perfect and constant peace*
> *whose inclination and character is stayed on Thee,*
> *without one ripple of anxiety, the mind of the one*
> *leaning hard upon me."* Isaiah 26:3

Doesn't this promise sound so idealistic as to be impossible? Especially with changes in medicine causing unrest...uncertainty of circumstances...burdens of anxiety...pessimism about the future.

To find relief, millions of intense people have given themselves to gulping "happy pills." Peace pills! These tired, nervous, fearful, and fretting patients have a "Do Not Disturb" sign on the door of their hearts. These drugs called ataraxics (Greek term meaning "not disturbed") have a way of screening out feelings of worry, fear, and anxiety. They are wonderful. They work

...for a while.

"Permanent Peace...can never be purchased.

Worry *is...spiritual irritability with Jesus."* —Oswald Chambers

Christian peace ultimately is not found in a pill…not in prosperity…nor in some place…rather **in the person and presence of God Himself.** He will guard what you give Him. Give.

Can the child of God ever think of anything the Heavenly Father will forget? When we realize that we could never think of anything He will forget

…**Worry** becomes impossible.

A woman kept a "Worry box" in her kitchen. Every time something troubled her, she would write it down and put it in the box. She resolved she would give these problems no thought as long as they were in the box. Often, she opened it and took out the slips of paper to review the concerns. She found her relaxed frame of mind enabled her to find solutions. She discovered to her delight that most of the troubles she worried about no longer existed!

Most of us are blown about by winds of circumstances, directed by gusts of passion, like a ship at sea with nobody at the helm. If your life is to be steady, there must be not only a strong hand at the helm but a fixed star for you to aim for…a harbor of rest.

When we put our cares in God's hands…
He puts His peace in our hearts.

Oh, if I trust Jesus, I will worry, but wait…I won't have worries!

"Never a test that He is not there, never a burden
He does not bear. Never a sorrow He does not share,
Moment by Moment…I am under His care." —Daniel W. Whittle

TEACHABLE SPIRIT

"We all want to learn, but we all hate to be taught." —Winston Churchill

Every person who aspires to top performance must be willing to accept suggestions for constructive change. From the cradle to the grave, an open heart to gentle reproof is an absolute.

"Better is a poor and wise youth than an old and foolish king…who

no longer knows how to receive friendly reproof and warning."
Ecclesiastes 4:13

The verse above tells about two personalities in contrast: a poor and wise child...and an old and foolish king! Which of the two would you rather have on your team? **God chooses the child. Why?**

"Become as little children..."

Children are teachable, malleable, and genuinely humble in heart. They most often are not impressed by their own importance or by tradition, nor are they victims of ritual and calloused independence.

The foolish king has lowered the throne beneath the highchair. The quality that propelled him to the top has departed. Why?

"He gives admonition by the bucketful, but accepts it by the grain!"

Can the surgeon take advice from the anesthesiologist, the dentist from the dental assistant? Humility is seeing the grace of God, who bought the mortgage on your life and paid the bills completely.

Live in light of the free grace...a sovereign gift that is unmerited, undeserved, unending...provided for every contingency.

Job was humbled. He did not need justice but mercy. God met Job when he had nothing...deserved nothing...and God promised him everything.

"Grace is love stooping...grace is love...out loving love."

Grace is not something but Someone. Grace is divine energy in the quest of unlovely men.

A humble one can claim with Paul "My grace is sufficient for you...My strength is made perfect in your weakness."

At this point in your life, have you discovered it is not enough to have money or knowledge, to climb the ladder of society, or even to have respect from your colleagues? When life seems but "a breath"...**God's grace is sufficient; it is enough!**

How do you know if you have humility? Are you an Attending or an Attentive?

Do you respond positively to reprimand and criticism?

Do you seek out the counsel of others and then with an open heart seek to make changes?

Do you harbor resentment toward those who are seeking to help you?

Admonition is like a red light. It is a warning of danger ahead. A humble person will listen to counsel.

"We all want to learn, but we all hate to be taught."

God's grace is sufficient!

———•••———

ANGER

Anger is a response to wounded love.

In your drive to get ahead…to lead the pack…to forge to the front, have you missed the force that makes life different? Impact and power does not come from jamming the accelerator of your life to the floorboard nor from forming a committee with the purpose of "Let's do something." The medical/dental field pace is excitingly fast. Everywhere is great scientific achievement. There is fear in every sensitive heart. . . there is driven-ness, lack of satisfying emotions, increase of unreason, rebellion, loss of control that has existed, and easy dismissal of the spiritual as being irrelevant.

"Most men live their lives in quiet desperation…" —Henry David Thoreau

Gnawing loneliness and vague, intense bitterness exists, besides the eternal fact that success and security come not from haste and hurry but from quietness and stillness.

Look back over your shoulder at the time-consuming pressures of recent weeks, the pursuit for position, the drive from money and power, the thirst for satisfaction and security. Has it been worth it all? We react with anger to all the demands that others—but especially we—place on ourselves. If your finger is on the panic button and exhaustion has you gasping for oxygen, learn the secret of "backing off." Psalm 46:10 says, **"Be still and know that I am God."** Give yourself time to be silent and quiet before Him, waiting to receive through the Holy Spirit assurance of His presence with you, His power working in you.

The power of stillness comes as you are willing to withdraw. . . to disengage yourself from much of the barrenness of busyness.

"Take time…you'll never have it until you take it." —Andrew Murray

To overcome the rush of anger, be still and know that God is God. Anger produces a disquieted spirit within your soul, a noisy restlessness that displays itself in grumbling, murmuring, and of all things fits of complaining. "How come this has happened to me?"

Decreasing stock or bank accounts…oil crises…a dark outlook for your practice and home makes you a candidate for a disquieted spirit.

Often the people who have climbed to tremendous heights take a nosedive into the slough of despondency. "The bigger they are, the harder they fall." The answer?

> *"Hope thou in God for I shall yet praise Him for the help of His countenance."* Psalm 42:5

Don't magnify your anger or sorrows. The tiny little bee has a miracle magnifying glass built in…its eyes multiply whatever it looks at into enormous numbers. The Israelite men's bee-attitude resulted in them saying, "They're giants and we're but grasshoppers!" (Numbers 13:33)

Not so for Caleb and Joshua. They saw their problems and impossibilities, but they also saw God. Their perspective was that God was between them and their problems.

Be still…magnify God not your problems.

—•••—

HEART

> *"Watch…over your heart with all diligence,*
> *for out of it flow the springs of life."*
> Proverbs 4:23

Do you use this principle and this promise? If you watch over your heart and do it with diligence, it will produce life. According to the Bible, thinking exists in the heart, and that is the region in which the Spirit of God deals. Jesus Christ never answers a question that springs from a man's head. The questions that spring from our brains are always borrowed from some book we've read, or someone we've heard speak, but the questions that spring from our hearts—the real problems that vex us—Jesus answers. These problems may be difficult to say in words, but they are the problems that Jesus will solve.

The heart is the center of living. God wants to bring perfect unity to spirit, soul, and body. The world, flesh, and devil seek also to give conscious unity to man's heart. The person who gives way to sensuality, worldliness, covetousness, is perfectly satisfied without God. God calls that **idolatry**.

The only way to alter the hardened heart is to melt it, and the only power that can melt it is the fire of the Holy Spirit. The heart is the altar of which other physical body is the outer court. Whatever is offered on the altar of the heart will ultimately manifest through the extremities of the body.

Impurity of heart will arise from various causes. Sometimes it comes through the open door of love and leaps down to the dark underground cellar of unlawful desire. The fire of impurity may be lit by the torch of pornographic books, which cause the mind to burn with desire, leaving behind the smoke of remorse and blackness of defeat. A thought, a look, a reach, a touch…involvement…depression!

Just like X-rays, the sensitive plate of the heart may photograph some scene upon it. The evil beast of impurity will eat the flowers of grace in our hearts unless we keep the gate of the soul's garden locked by **"powerful watching."** Impurity closes the eyes to the vision of God, for it's only the pure in heart who see Him (Matthew 5:8). Impurity diverts the purpose of God, for the end of His commandment is love from a pure heart (1 Timothy 1:5). Impurity paralyzes the hand of faith, for faith is to be held with a pure conscience (1 Timothy 3:9). Impurity takes away the appetite for spiritual things (Titus 1:15).

How are you doing in "watching your heart with all diligence"? Do you need help? A suggestion: Find someone who will in love hold you accountable. Ask him or her to help you "fix your eyes on Jesus, the author and finisher of our faith."

Keep watching your heart!

HIS OWN PLACE

Imagine. Judas walked with Christ along with the other disciples for over three years. He felt "out of place" with them. It took the traumatic events of the final week to reveal his true character.

> *"You Lord, who know the hearts of all, show which one of these two you have chosen to take the place in this ministry and apostleship*

from which Judas turned aside...to go to his own place. *Acts 1:24-25*

Where are you most comfortable: in the company of Bible-believing Christians or with a Bible-doubting majority that has chosen to ignore God? Then your "own place" will surely be with them in the future life. Such a person would be more miserable in heaven than in "his own place." At death, each of us will go to his own place...whether heaven or hell.

"Resist beginnings that have damning conclusions."

Successful fruitage depends upon solid rootage. A prideful heart can go on for years unnoticed because the root was repressed, suppressed, or oppressed...but never killed. We must smother the roots of doubt, despair, or discouragement. Do not fan the flames—it will spread.

The root of bitterness grew rapidly in the hearts of the Israelites in the wilderness. They murmured against the grace of God. They complained they had no water, no food. God gave them manna from heaven. They then complained that it was so bland! They sowed the seed of discontent...their families reaped the harvest of a natural disaster. Why not cut the roots of bitterness and an unforgiving spirit.

The root of pride in the heart of Solomon manifested in the later years. As long as he viewed himself as low in his own sight, he kept to the path of obedience. When he became enamored over his own importance as King, he turned aside into pride. He lost his kingdom. When the ambition of pride rides upon us it will ride us to death...if it can or stoop to anything in order to gain its end.

A prideful person is an angry person...a critical person. Pride is so keen to detect pride in others. The reason is, it wants what makes the other proud. The root of pride in Jonah caused him to run from the revelation God gave him of Ninevah. The great fish story returns him from his physical rebellion, but he ends up saying, "Don't I have a right to be angry?" He was angry because of God's overwhelming mercy and grace. What makes you angry?

Pride takes the soul out of humility...the brightness out of joy...the life out of love... love out of prayer...the grip out of faith.

An artificial profession of belief, like that of Judas, will not change one's basic character. Sooner or later that person will be found all together "out of place." A true change of heart by genuine faith in Christ will change our eternal residence, because God has said he would deliver us from the power of darkness and translate us into the kingdom of His dear Son (Colossians 1:13).

Jesus said, "Let not your heart be troubled. I go to prepare a place for you." Jesus has prepared a wonderful place for those who truly desire to be with Him…in His place. What reservations are you making today for your future?

Do you have your "own place" or will you be in "His place"?

— •••—

ADVERSITY

If God has made your cup sweet, drink it with grace; if He has made it bitter, drink it in communion with Him.

> *"For our light, momentary affliction is ever more and more abundantly preparing and producing and achieving for us an everlasting weight of glory—beyond all measure, excessively surpassing all comparisons and all calculations, a vast and transcendent glory and blessedness… never to cease!"* 2 Corinthians 4:17

"Our light affliction…" To escape affliction is a cowardly thing to do; to seek relief is natural; to draw closer to God through it is a spiritual thing. Most of us have tried the first, a good many of us have known the second, and the Spirit of God in us knows the third. . . getting through "to the eternal weight of glory."

God never promised to keep us immune from trouble. Even in a hurricane? Yes, **"I will be with him in trouble"**…and that is a very different thing!

John Newton compared the troubles we have in the course of a year to a great bundle of sticks far too large for us to lift. God does not require us to carry the whole bundle at once. He mercifully unties the bundle and gives us first one stick, which we are to carry today, and then another, which we are to carry tomorrow, and so on. This we might easily manage if we would take only the burden appointed for us each day; but we choose to increase our troubles by carrying yesterday's stick over again today and reaching out and adding tomorrow's burden to our load…before we are required to bear it.

The world owes much to sorrow. Why? Most of the Psalms were born in a wilderness. Many of the Epistles were written from a prison. The greatest poets have learned in suffering what they taught in song. Have you had patients who have complained and given you sorrow?

"When God is about to make great use of a person, He puts them in the fire."

We learn wisdom from failure more than from success. We often discover which operations will work by learning which will not. Great thoughts, medical discoveries, and inventions have generally been nurtured in hardship...often pondered over in sorrow and established with difficulty. As the tree is fertilized by its own broken branches and fallen leaves and it then grows out of its decay, so people are improved by trial...refined out of broken hopes...and blighted expectations.

Among some skaters was a small boy, evidently a beginner. His frequent falls awakened the pity of a tender-hearted spectator. "Why, sonny, you're getting all banged up!" she said. "I wouldn't stay on the ice and keep falling down. I would just come off and watch the others." While the tears of the last fall were rolling down over his rosy cheeks, the child looked from his advisor to the shining steel on his feet and answered, half-indignantly, **"I didn't get some new skates to give up with; I got them to learn how with."**

Life's hard tasks are never sent for us to **"give up with."** They are always intended to awaken strength and skill...to encourage in learning how to master them.

A musician is not remembered for playing long but for playing well; God wants willing obedience and not forced service. Cain served God grudgingly. He brought his sacrifice, not his heart. God does not want to beat good works out of us as the water came out of the rock when Moses struck it with his rod, but He wants our loving service to drop as honey...from a honeycomb and water...from a faucet.

Do you hurt as you see your children hurt from the pathology you passed on from your parents...the judgments you made, the sowing and reaping of generational sins? Remember...God hurt with His Son when He was put on the cross.

If God has made your cup sweet, drink it with grace.

If God has made your cup bitter, drink it in communion with Him.

———•••———

FEAR AND ENCOURAGEMENT

Look at the	Problem	and	Solution in Isaiah 41:10
	"Do not Fear		"I AM" with you
	Do not be Dismayed		"I AM" your God
	I will Strengthen		You
	I will Help		You
	I will Uphold		You with My righteous right hand."

Fear

Notice, there is a tangible, emotional problem…Fear! But even more wonderful there is God's solution. His Presence. (I AM with you [face to face] and His Person [I AM your God], The Great I Am of Moses.)

The Greater the problem, the greater is the felt solution.

I have been fearful and dismayed (being an obsessive-compulsive) as I created my own responsibilities, e.g., Medical Couples (Monday night), Single Medical School men and women (Tuesday night), Pizza & Perspective, Counseling Physicians (5:15–6:30am), multiple administrative requirements, planning strategies and objectives, raising funds for salaries, retreats, Summer Medical Institute (June-July), fulfilling reports needed at Briarwood, performing marriages, funerals, praying, studying the Word, teaching and loving those who never had a father, trying to get sleep, trying to get up, helping my grown children, reaching out to a grandson in Montreal (many miles away)…BUT, I am encouraged by seeing who God really is as I study the Names of God and His Attributes. He really is my Yhwh…Shammah. God is there…and here as I write.

Trust God's heart, even if you can't see God's hand.

Encouragement

Definition: Judy, my wife, is a gift of God, the epitome of encouragement as many receive her Hug Therapy. Do you know how privileged I am to be deeply loved…unconditionally, having a wonderful wife and many deep friends?

One physician recently said he had friends in college but no one close to him now. He once said, "How could someone as old as you be my best friend!" I'm being drawn in to be an encouragement to him and I'm so glad.

Encouragement is a balm to discouraged spirits and a tonic to the downhearted. Someone has said that people are like corn—they will live if planted with the necessary cultivation, sunshine, and TLC.

Encouragement is like penicillin to the younger professionals having lived with deferred gratification. When losing their grip on life, they need a load lifter/bearer, not destructive criticism or sarcasm.

I'm still "running the race with endurance, fixing my eyes on Jesus," praying I'll be more like David. He was in a cave; Saul sought to kill him. Gossip was running hot, some people were in an angry mood, and then David makes this majestic statement:

"But David encouraged himself, in the Lord his God." 1 Samuel 30:6

If the Trinity stopped thinking of me, they would cease to exist.

The ultimate encourager is God our Abba, Jesus our Joint Heir, and the Holy Spirit (paraclete), called alongside to comfort the uncomfortable.

Be encouraged and do not fear!

———•••———

TENSION

How do you live the Christian life?

My mentor, Dr. Howard Hendricks, taught me that most people are people of extremes. They are out on the fringes. The Scriptures demonstrate the Holy Spirit is balanced, in the middle. Truth to be embraced must be overstated to move the person from the far right or left to a center position. **How do you live the Christian life?** Look at the last sentence of this essay. It is not a question, but it is the answer.

I have books on both sides of this controversy; people have only stated one position and ignored the other. For instance, "the Christian life is not difficult to live, but it is impossible…it is a supernatural life." That is a true truth adequately stated in the first part of the verse in Galatians 2:20:

"I have been crucified with Christ. It is no longer I who live but Christ who lives in me."

However, this doesn't say all the Scriptures say. Man's responsibility is to live "by Faith in the Son of God, the object of Faith." Jesus in the flesh, Jesus…full of Grace and Truth. There it is! Grace and Truth…not one to the exclusion of the other but a both/and. We can not accept God's tension, so we are constantly trying to resolve it by overemphasizing God's sovereignty and/or human responsibility.

How did Jesus live the Christian life? We find Him dependant, in prayer, tired, hungry, sweating, with no place to lay His head (seemed like He liked camping a lot); to the opposite extreme, He didn't need to have anyone instruct Him…for He knew what is in man. In one moment, He operated out of His humanity, and the next moment He operates out of His Deity. Theologians are uncomfortable with this. How could this be? Explain to me how a God could come in the flesh and send His only Son to die for someone like you and me! Explain the measure of that love and grace.

"The measure of love…is that 'it' cannot 'be' measured." —Thomas Merton

How do you live the Christian life? Both…supernatural and natural. Let go and move out. As it was explained by a deep theologian while boating in Destin, when my son was a 10-year-old: "Dad, when you are in a storm. . . pray to God and row to shore."

How do you live the Christian life? You live in tension. It is 100% of what God does. Christ lives His life through me supernaturally. He loves the unlovely, He forgives the unforgivable, He knows the unknowable, He hurts with the hurting, He helps the helpless. He stands between the poor and the unprotected, He lifts up the downtrodden, He heals the brokenhearted…and He does all that supernaturally…at the very same moment it is 100% of what we do!

You give a cup of cold water, you teach a Bible study, you change a diaper! All of the power of God is in that moment. The human responsibility is living by faith.

What will you do today? Live by faith in the Son of God…expecting the supernatural…mystical…wonderfully overwhelming…overflowing power of Jesus. Loving Him with your heart, thinking with your mind, speaking with your lips, laughing with your eyes…

Welcome to tension.

— •••—

LONELINESS

"I am like a melancholy pelican of the wilderness; I am like a desolate owl of the waste places. I am sleepless and lie awake like a bereaved sparrow." Psalm 102:67

Have you ever felt in the pit of your stomach the results of being lonely? You're in a crowd, around a crowd, you are the crowd; you have friends, family, patients to treat, responsibilities to execute...but you feel lonely. **Where does loneliness come from?**

Many people are lonely because they've been hurt. They don't want to *risk* further relationships.

The most severe loneliness is often caused by rejection. Those who need friendship the most are sometimes the most rejected because of their personality...or parents... or lack of social graces. Often those who come into the dental and medical field have tendencies toward being an introvert. Judy and I see students who want to live alone... and be left alone.

When you're a perfectionist, isn't it hard to find someone who will ever measure up to being a roommate? We're fortunate that God has built in attraction to the opposite sex or we might not ever find one—for love overlooks faults. Many of these get married, but maintain their loneliness. Their spouses end up with emotions that are starved. As one resident spouse said, "I'm tired of being a roommate and not a wife."

The three kinds of animals mentioned above don't flock together; they're loners. The pelican is a mournful bird that will sit motionless for hours. The horned owls not only are unclean creatures but are fond of the loneliness of the desert. They can sit glued to their perch, never moving unnecessarily and giving out a low wailing note. Lastly, the lonesome bird that sits on top of the house while all are asleep and gives a monotonous sound of melancholy is not found to associate with others.

Solution? Jesus promised His presence in Matthew 28:20, saying, "Lo, **I am with you** always." Have you felt the presence...of God's omnipresence? There's no spot that you can go where God is not! Be alone with God. Alone...but never alone!

That's the vertical. How about the horizontal? Proverbs 18:24 says, *"A man of many friends comes to ruin, but there's a friend who sticks closer than a brother."* The word "friend" means one who loves, and one who "sticks" is someone who shoulders something together. It is the image of the breastplate. To have a friend, you need to be a friend. Galatians 6:4 shows the sowing/reaping principle—if you sow friendship, you're going to reap friendship. If you sow love, you're going to reap love. Is there risk doing that? Yes! I've found there is no capacity to love without the capacity to be hurt.

The trials of life such as a spouse moving out, children in rebellion, and financial complications are instituted by God to make you realize that you really need Him. In those times, James 1:2 says, *"Consider it all joy when you face various trials."* Maybe this is the time for you to set aside a day, two days, to pray, fast, and be alone with your personal Savior, listen to Him, love Him…because He first loved you. Then return to the heat of the battle, because you're not alone.

"Loneliness is a signal that it's time for us to become better acquainted with God."

---•••---

TO RUSSIA WITH LOVE

Back in the mid '90s I spent twelve dependent days at medical schools in Kirov and Tver, Russia. I was "dependent" to get through customs with eleven boxes of drugs (they kept three) and on the exciting flight over Greenland and Europe, finally landing in Moscow. All my life I had heard of the Red Square. I finally stood, as it began to drizzle, on the stones that soldiers had marched in cadence with each other. To a Russian nearby I shared, "If you went to Jesus' tomb He is not there because He has risen. Lenin is in his tomb."

What an exciting adventure with a fourteen-hour train ride in a Pullman compartment car from Moscow to Kirov! This event reminded me of movies I had seen during World War II. As we stopped at cities en route and I stepped off of the platform, I had the same feelings. Our team stayed at the KGB hotel that had been built exclusively for them. Laughingly, we wondered if our conversations were being recorded! We felt safe since three soldiers were in the lobby at all times.

We were hosted by the head of the Department of Pharmacology, Dr. Valdislav Zaugolnikov, for tea soon after faculty and students met us in 14-degree weather at the train station and escorted us to the Kirov Medical Institute.

Little did I realize how I would be giving talks up to five times each day and the people of whom I was just now meeting were going to become close personal friends. For seventy years they had a course of Atheism and Communism, and now that teaching time is open to someone such as myself to give lectures on Medical Ethics and how to take care of your personal life as a medical professional. Students were not used to my method of teaching: I moved into the aisles of the class, I touched them, and I asked their names and for their opinions. The professor told me that they were not used to having an instructor be so personal—to speak to their emotions not just their intellect.

I was challenged to communicate through our translator. I spent so much time with her I grew to be fond of Valaria. She was at the University of Moscow studying English at the age of 18 years old (though she looked 24). She came from a divorced home. As the week developed, she would affectionately call me Papa. Maybe this was the reason that I was sent to Russia…to share my feelings of overwhelming love and affection toward her as a father would to a daughter?

The faculty was thankful for the sutures and antibiotics that I had been given by local doctors here with which to bless them. That was particularly true of Sergei, a Russian dermatologist who was head of the S.T.D. clinic there. Since they do not have long-acting antibiotics, they have to give antibiotics every four hours in patients to deal with sexually transmitted diseases. It was deeply satisfying to meet a very specific need.

I had never really realized that I would be so far from my home and yet pressed so close to Jesus that I found Him squeezing His love out of me and into them. It is so true that love never fails. **Love is a language that communicates beyond any translation.**

We went in love, and we received love. Jesus continued to love His own so much so that John stated, **"He loved them to the end"** (John 13:1). **His love knew no bounds…never wore thin…never reached the end of its tether.** Only hours before a cruel hand seized Him to torture Him, He paused to draw near to the Father to pray on behalf of His disciples.

Jesus did not ask on behalf of the disciples alone but also for those of us who would believe in Him through their word. Even though we have come centuries later, we know He loved us enough to intercede for us.

> *"Love that goes upward is worship. Love that goes outward is affection. Love that stoops is grace. On that dark night en route to Gethsemane, Jesus stooped in grace to pray for His own."*
> —Donald Barnhouse

Our trip was a manifestation of God's love: physical, emotional, and spiritual. God blessed us by sending us **to Russia…with love**!

••••

INGRATITUDE OF LOVED ONES

How does a person handle rebellion or rejection? From his family?

> *"For the enemy has persecuted my soul.*
> *He has crushed my life to the ground. . .*
> *Therefore, my spirit is overwhelmed within me.*
> *My Heart within me is Distressed"* Psalm 143:3-4

David's song is very clear that he knew something of troubles…trials…rejections we have. David the king was fleeing from Jerusalem because of Absalom, his son!

Note the expression he uses to describe the opposition—the enemy persecutes…crushes…my heart is distressed…the deep melancholy mourning of a dethroned King by his own son, his own flesh who he loves deeply, who has crushed him. David is so overwhelmed feeling banishment, lonely, perplexed, afraid, forsaken of God to escape towards death.

"To have been hurt much, indicates you have loved much."

You will never be hurt so much unless you have loved. There is no love without self-giving. There is no self-giving without pain. Therefore, there is no love without suffering. Even God didn't love without cost. Think what it must have cost Him to give His Son as a sin offering on the cross, and then to forsake, turn His face away from His innocent Son. Separation…a moment of eternal pain. Unfathomable!

We are the bride-elect being taught the lessons of "agape" love in preparation for living in God's throne room. Deep dimensions of love are learned in the school of suffering and testing. Purity is one thing, and maturity is another.

But, in the midst of the storm, David remembers his God!

> *"I Remember…the days of old.*
> *I Meditate…on all thy doings.*
> *I Muse…on the work of thy hand.*
> *I Stretch…out my hands to Thee."* Psalm 143:5,6

Meditation is…prayer's handmaid to wait on it.

It is the plow before the sower sows, prepares it.

It is the harrow after…to cover it.

David knows that beyond the clouds, the sun is "always shining." This I know to be true, too, but how difficult it is to see God because of the magnitude of the storms.

David felt the abandonment by his son. So, as he escapes, he realizes that

> *"Past memories are as flowers for the bees of faith to make honey for your present use."*

The past shows a reservoir of folly to be avoided and wisdom to be loved. Remember God's past faithfulness with expectant hope for the future. How do you live in the present moment? Eat the Honey!

What was the secret of David's making lemonade out of such a basketful of lemons?

He had one desire: to know God intimately. When you know God, you view storms/rejection differently. Circle these words in Psalm 143.

> **"Hear my prayer**
> **…give ear,**
> **…answer me speedily,**
> **…cause me to hear your loving kindness in the morning,**
> **…deliver me,**
> **…revive me.**

The disciples in the terrible storm on the Sea of Galilee thought they were going to drown…"the boat was in the water, but the water was in the boat!" They awoke Jesus from a deep sleep, saying, "Don't you care? We are perishing." They forgot:

> *"With Christ in the vessel, you can smile at the storm."* —Dr. Scotty Morris

God is using personality clashes, unjust criticism, financial reverses, physical affliction, personal hostilities of the family, even old age as "on the job" training to learn deeper lessons of agape love as the currency of eternity.

Don't resist…resolve…to let agape flow by faith in the only Faithful one…**JESUS, JESUS**!

> *"We are not here to make an impact but to give away love."* —Brennan Manning

——•••——

CAST YOUR BURDENS

Trials, traumas, crises…

What do they do to us?

They collapse our world view, shatter our assumptions about life, and cause us to question our faith…in our God and ourselves.

They can leave us in the black hole of despair and depression.

When they hit, our sense of invulnerability is attacked. It reminds us that we are terribly mortal and vulnerable. When they hit, our rationality is thrown to the wind, our world no longer makes sense, our moral sense is challenged. The world no longer seems just and fair.

What do you do when the burden gets too heavy? When you're swamped, do you "Flee!" or "Fight!"? Battle it out…be tough…change circumstances. What do you do? "CAST!"

> *"Cast your burden on the Lord and He will sustain you; He will never allow the righteous to be pushed over."* Psalm 55:22

His name is Comforter, Burden-Bearer. The Hebrew means "the portion assigned to you." That which God in His gracious supervision feels to be your allotment.

Are you facing the tragedy of a child who sows to the wind, soon to reap the whirlwind? The treachery of a trusted colleague…the load of financial pressure…the inequality of cost schedules, vacations, and expectations.

Do you have crippling anxieties, a sharp thorn of sorrow that you can't share with another living soul?

What must we do? CAST.

What does God promise to do? SUSTAIN.

He didn't promise to remove the burden, but He did promise to sustain you (comfort and strengthen the inner garrison of your soul). Not only does He carry the burden, but also He carries us!

Trials, traumas, crises…what do they do to us? The same thing they did to Job, the

Psalmist, Elijah. For Elijah found out that in serving "in the will of God, the brook dries up." Elijah prayed for no rain and guess what? His answered prayer meant no rain for him, but God told him to drink from the Kerith Brook and eat what the ravens bring. Then the brook dried up. But God sent him to a widow of Zarephath, whose cup of water and small supply of flour and oil fed them for three years.

Paul, who had been in prison, beaten, in danger of death, shipwrecked, and robbed, was without sleep, food, and clothes as stated in 2 Corinthians 11:23. He also realized Jesus' burden-carrying words: "My grace is sufficient for you" for my power is perfected… in weakness (2 Corinthians 12:9). Here is a providential paradox: Tragedy and trust are often linked together in the plan of God.

Darkness came before light is as sure as God, Himself. Look at the Ruthless Trusters of God's faithfulness so completely demonstrated in Hebrews 11. They lived in the truth of His faithfulness.

> *"All of God's greats have been weak people, who did great exploits for God because they reckoned on His being faithful."* —Hudson Taylor

Abraham's wife, Sarah (age 90), hearing that she was going to birth a promised son, laughed in the face of God. It was impossible. It couldn't happen! Then she came to the realization that if He is to be trusted at all, then she is to trust Him with all. Isaac = laughter.

> **"She could do this because she believed that the One who had given the promise was utterly trustworthy."** Hebrews 11:11

Will you exchange your instability for His faithfulness?

> **"Let God be true and every man a liar."** Romans 3:4

Cast all your cares on the Rock…which is Jesus.

— •••

STONES

Getting stoned…The Rolling Stones…gall stones…kidney stones…smooth stones…stones of remembrance…living stones.

Have you ever visited an inlet of the sea that reached into the land, leaving a sheltered bay? The pebbles on that protected beach are rough and jagged not smooth and polished. Out on the open shore where fierce breakers roar over the rocks, the resultant pebbles are sleek, smooth, and round. So it is with Christian character. Just as the harsh treatment of the ocean waves makes the rough stones smooth, so our trials, difficulties, and testings can produce in us the luster of Christian maturity.

"The testing of your faith produces patience." James 1:3

Stones of Remembrance. A stack of twelve large stones stood in a heap. They had been taken from the Jordan when Joshua and the Hebrews crossed over the riverbed en route to Jericho. God had dried up the river so that his people could cross over as He had done with the Red Sea forty years earlier. Therefore, Joshua was instructed to leave a stack of stones on the shore as a remembrance for generations to come. Their future children would ask, "What do these stones mean?" They were told of God's mighty acts; be encouraged to worship Him forever! God wants us to recognize that He is "solid as stone" to remind us that based on His attributes we may have our respect for Him glorified, our praise to Him magnified.

Stones of the Ten Commandments. God took two pieces of stone, and with His own finger He wrote on them the Ten Commandments, which would shake and shape the world with its implications. Making something out of nothing is a continual pattern of God.

Michelangelo could take a 50-cent piece of canvas, paint a picture on it, and make it worth thousands of dollars—that is art. But God could take a 40-year-old, conceited person named Moses, and give him forty years to learn he was nobody, then allow him another forty years to discover what God could do with anybody—that is patience!

Where we go in a time of trial proves what the great underlying power in our lives is. Our treasure in Heaven is faith…that has been tried on Earth. If our treasure is in Heaven, we don't need to persuade ourselves that it is; we prove that it is by the way we deal with matters on Earth.

Living Stones. Doesn't that sound like a contradiction? We have the life of Jesus, the cornerstone, living in us in supernatural ways. The Christian life is not difficult to live…it's impossible.

> *"In coming to Him as to a 'living stone' rejected by men but choice and precious in the sight of God, you also as 'living stones' are being built up as a spiritual house for a holy priesthood to offer up spiritual sacrifices acceptable to God through Jesus Christ."* 1 Peter 2:4-5

Through the rough season of our difficulties, God is in the process of "rounding" the stones of our character. He is conforming us to the likeness of His son. Getting stoned… The Rolling Stones…gall stones…kidney stones…or smooth and living stones—which are you?

•••

THE CERTAINTY OF UNCERTAINTY

The nature of spiritual life is that we are certain in our uncertainty. If this is true, then we do not make a "nest" out of a profession or a creed or a belief.

Immediately when I become certain, something dies. For instance, when I become certain that my grandbaby (Julien) is no longer a baby but now a little boy, the baby is "dead." When I become certain that a single medical school student is now married, something is "dead." If I become certain of my creeds, I end up killing the life of God in my soul because I cease to believe in God…and believe in my belief instead.

The thing I love about the Bible is it is a paradox. The realm of the uncertain is the realm of joy and delight. Why is that?

"The certainty of God means uncertainty in life."

I have always been big on written goals, objectives, and plans. I also have wanted to be careful and certain in the next step. I now find, when I am gloriously uncertain of the next step, then I am certain of God.

When I immediately abandon myself to God and do what lies nearest to me, He packs my life with surprises all the time.

The older I get the more childlike I want to become, since Jesus said…

"Become like little children…"

Look at the expectant wonder of children; **see a little child certain of its parents but uncertain of everything else.** Therefore, it lives a perfectly delightful, healthy life. Oh, to be a child again!

What do you feel uncertain about? Fast-breaking changes are occurring with the healthcare landscape, Medicare reimbursement, personnel…your spouse. You are recruited by a professional managerial group or hospital to join. The initial salary looks better. Your location entitles you to a bonus. Then…that which seemed certain becomes uncertain. A year later they need to cut you 20% to "be competitive." You look back at the special ski trip to Vail, you look forward to your new mortgage you received with the new house.

What can you count on? What if you were counting on drinking living water from "the Rock, who is Christ," who never changes?

> **"And all drank the same spiritual drink, for they were drinking from a spiritual rock which followed them; and the rock was Christ."**
> 1 Corinthians 10:4

What effect does this have on me? Will our receiving funds decrease? Where can we cut back? What if…? Where will I find certainty?

Here it is…

> **"Therefore, we do not lose heart, but though our outer man is decaying, yet our inner man is being renewed day by day. For momentary, light affliction is producing for us an eternal weight of glory far beyond all comparison, while we look not at the things which are seen, but at the things which are not seen; for the things which are seen are temporal, but the things which are not seen are eternal."**
> 2 Corinthians 4:16-18

Looking at the unseen…the eternal…certain in my uncertainty.

— ••• —

TRIALS

"Do not fear for I have redeemed you; I have called you by name; you are mine! When you pass through the waters, I will be with you; And through the rivers, they will not overflow you. When you walk through the fire, you will not be scorched, nor will the flames burn you. For I am the Lord your God...since you are precious in my sight, you are honored and I love you...do not fear, for I am with you." Isaiah 43:1-4

The trials and difficulties are not to be evaded but encountered. Don't run from them, but, by God's sustaining grace, run through them. God says not to be afraid, for He is with us, and because of this we are to go through the perplexities of life. In God's economy conflicts are not the end but a means. He is more interested in the process than the product—how do we walk in the way, not just our arrival? He's not as interested in the conclusion as He is in our condition—a pause but certainly not the final period. Note how we go through the three items...through the waters not alone, through rivers not swamped, through fires not harmed.

Do you feel like you are in a frying pan? Remember Daniel in that lion's den, King Saul chased David, God's anointed Elijah contended alone for God on Mount Carmel, Gideon's army was reduced to merely 300 men. You never feel so alone, till you feel God promise that you are not alone.

"Some of you pass through the waters, some pass through the flood, some into the fire, but all are saved through the blood. Some experience great sorrow, but God sings the song in the morning of early darkness, in the twilight of the day long (He gives) fresh courage and strength."

Encouragement is like penicillin. When a person's heart is down and his feet are dragging and his spirits are low, how wonderful it is to have a person speak words of encouragement especially when it is Jesus. Take courage. You are serving Christ.

——•••——

HELP

"When the world has gotten you down
you feel rotten, in a big hurry
too doggone tired to pray
and

you're mad at everybody
…**HELP!**

Why is it such a struggle for us to cry out for assistance?

The surgeons will arrange for help in extensive or intricate operations.

Ants do it all the time—look at the load they carry together! No sport is won without substitutions. (Off-the-bench players often win the games.)

Asking for help is smart…the answer to fatigue, and the "indispensable image" that blocks you from asking for help is **PRIDE.**

The breeding ground of high-achieving parents as well as high-pressure competition in professional schools and residencies bring that inner voice…urging us to prove it to them.

The result? A lifestyle of impatience…

We become easily irritated…often angry
…work long hours
…take less time off
…forget how to laugh
…cancel vacations
…enjoy fewer and fewer moments in prayer.

The Answer: You don't have to hack it alone!

The LORD your God is with you, He is mighty to save. He will take great delight in you, He will quiet you with his love; He will rejoice over you with singing." Zephaniah 3:17

Jesus is not the Lord of the perimeter. Either He is dead center or there's trouble! In the middle of the Tabernacle was the Holy of Holies. God's presence. The Lord never planned a life where He is on the fringe. He is walking in my steps…feeling the heartbeat of every area of life.

Moses flashed from one need to another. From early morning until late night, the harried leader was knee-deep in decisions. Eating on the run, planning appointments, meeting deadlines. Impressive?

Jethro (the father-in-law) wasn't impressed. Jethro reproves him with strong words:

> **"The thing you are doing is not good. You will surely wear out."**
> Exodus 18:17

He told Moses to…

CALL FOR HELP

The Benefits?

> **"So it will be easier for you…you will be able to endure. If you do this, God will direct you, you will be able to endure…"** Exodus 18:22-23

Since when is a bleeding ulcer a sign of spirituality? Or no time off and a 70-hour week a mark of efficiency?

> *"Efficiency is enhanced not by what we accomplish, but by what we relinquish.*
> —Chuck Swindoll

God loves to hear us shout…when we are discouraged…for

HELP!

— ••• —

PAIN

"God whispers to us in our pleasures. . .but he shouts in our pains." —C.S. Lewis

Have you ever gotten tired of pain? I woke up one night at 2:30 a.m. with back pain… in a room with eight dental students in Costa Rica. My spirit was willing, but the body was weak! I lay there contemplating 30 years of the "pains" that I have seen. We are privileged to be involved with people who are in actuality…**Wounded Healers.** So many go into medicine and dentistry in order to numb their own pain from childhood.

Some of the students have been "in pain" because their parents have been perfectionists in the healthcare profession. Because of the training and on-call constraints, the parent was not there when they were young. Maybe…just maybe…in the midst of healing others, some healing would spill over into their lives. Jesus has sent to us many who, hearing messages from the void in their lives, are reaching and looking for an older mentor, believing he will deeply meet their needs.

I hear pain of one student's parent who had been through seven divorces, another through two. Some students have parents or loved ones who face cancer and terminal diseases.

How do you help those who are "in pain"? What is going to be effective in their lives? I realize the pain in my own life has equipped me to be broken, sensitive, and unable to have the formula. The joy is in sharing Jesus…listening…hurting with them…identifying wounds…praying for emotional healing. The Lord Jesus came **"to heal the brokenhearted…"** (Luke 4:18).

Why do you enjoy healing the sick? Don't you get tired of seeing only sick people? Where are the well ones? Just as you may lose patients to the throes of death, so we see the death of people shooting themselves in the foot by entering divorce. This wrenching of relationships compounds their pain, transfers it to children, and propagates the things they hate the most. If you don't change…you will replicate it again.

> *"We are born again by pain, not necessarily pain to ourselves any more than our natural birth means pain to us. We are born into the realm where our Lord lives…by pain to God and the pain of God is exhibited on…Calvary."* —Oswald Chambers

Like Paul, we are able to "sing in the pain." Isn't it an incredulous statement he makes to have been beaten, shipwrecked, persecuted, felt rejection, abandonment, and hatred from Jews and Gentiles? Paul's solace in pain is,

> "Nothing would ever separate him from the unconditional…
> Unmerited…relentless…furious…love of Jesus Christ."

This is why we are here. Not to medicate pain but to identify it…then allow Jesus to "heal" it. Pray Jesus will enable us to keep on keeping on to communicate the **beauty** of salvation, the **joy** of sanctification, and the certain expectation of **hope** in Christ Jesus.

Beauty…joy…hope…in pain!

———•••———

SEEING RED

"Fools give full vent to their rage, but the wise bring calm in the end."
Proverbs 29:11

"In your anger, do not sin." Ephesians 4:26

Throwing a chair across the basketball court…Slamming a fist through a wall… Showing frustration when someone cuts you off in traffic…Having those feelings you get when someone tells a trusted secret…Realizing how a child feels when dad doesn't come home. When life isn't the way we think it should be, it's easy to get angry. God wired us that way.

Anger is one of the most often misunderstood yet significant concepts in life. Best understood as "a state of preparedness" to respond to a real or perceived wrongdoing or injustice in life, anger motivates a person to action.

Paul taught in Ephesians 4:26 (NIV), **"In your anger, don't sin."** While anger always finds an expression, what you decide to do in your "state of preparedness" determines whether or not you will "sin."

Anger management starts when we:

See it—Identifying the cause of anger in your life especially opens your spirit for God's help. **"Likewise, the Spirit helps us in our weakness…" (Romans 8:26 ESV).**

Delay it—Learn the value of "calming" to allow the anger to subside. **"Whoever is slow to anger has great understanding, but he who has a hasty temper exalts folly"** (Proverbs 14:29 ESV).

Control it—Control your response rather than reacting emotionally. **"Better a patient person than a warrior, one with self-control than one who takes a city"** (Proverbs 16:32 NIV).

Settle it—Commit to not only "doing" the right things but also "being" the right person. **"Finally, all of you, be like-minded, be sympathetic, love one another, be compassionate and humble. Do not repay evil with evil or insult with insult. On the contrary, repay evil with blessing, because to this you were called so that you may inherit a blessing"** (1 Peter 3:8-9 NIV).

When you invite God to help you identify your anger and take positive action, anger becomes a servant rather than a master.

In your anger—choose not to sin. It just might turn your life around.

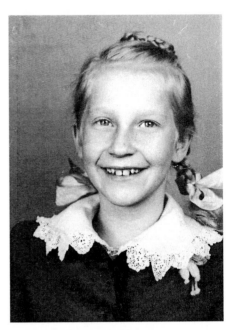

(TOP LEFT) Earle on his sixth birthday in a cowboy outfit his mom rented. (TOP RIGHT) Judy as an eight-year-old. (BOTTOM) Earle married Judy Spears on August 24, 1962, at Canterbury United Methodist Church in Mountain Brook, Alabama.

(TOP LEFT) Judy modeled in many advertisements in the 1960s. (TOP RIGHT) Earle, shown here in 1972, was Staff Leader for Campus Crusade at LSU for five years in the early 1970s. (BOTTOM LEFT) Judy and Earle in the late 1970s. (BOTTOM RIGHT) Earle and Judy with their children Missy and Conrad in 1978. This picture was used in a publication for the Dallas Theological Seminary, where Earle was a student at the time.

Vincet Ebby) Pam

(OPPOSITE) This is Judy's famous prayer list. She prayed for these people for more than 25 years—every day. (TOP) Earle (right) in 1998 with one of his greatest mentors, Brennan Manning, author of *The Ragamuffin Gospel*. Brennan spoke at numerous Christian Medical Ministry of Alabama (CMMA) events over the years. (BOTTOM) CMMA retreat at Lake Martin, hosted by Dr. and Mrs. Max Austin in the late 1990s.

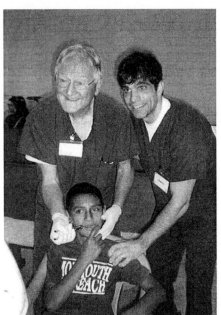
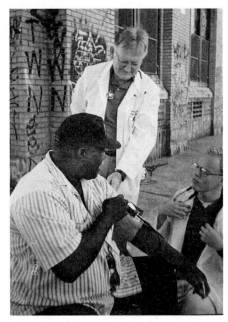

(TOP) Earle and Judy on a mid-1980s retreat to the Tennessee mountains with medical students Clay (and Tammy) Rowe, Bill Halama, and Carter (and Cindy) Harsh. (BOTTOM LEFT) Earle and Dr. Stephen Thomas on a CMMA mission trip to Costa Rica in the early 2000s. (BOTTOM RIGHT) For many summers in the 1990s, CMMA would send UAB medical students on a six-week mission to Philadelphia, Pennsylvania, where they would treat people of the Barrio physically and spiritually.

(TOP) In 1995 at a medical school in Tevr, Russia, where Earle was invited to speak to multinational medical students, Earle is pictured with Dr. Valdislav Zaugolnikov. See "To Russia with Love," page 83. (BOTTOM) Earle poses with members of the Maasai tribe on a CMMA mission trip to Kenya and Tanzania.

(TOP) Earle blesses a bride before the wedding ceremony. In CMMA circles, the quote was "Judy matches them up, and Earle marries them up!" (BOTTOM) The Carpenter family at the 30th anniversary of the Christian Medical Ministry in 2012: Judy, Missy, Kayin, Conrad, Wells, Earle, and Julien. (OPPOSITE) Earle and Judy celebrate their 60th wedding anniversary on August 24, 2022.

CHAPTER THREE

WORD

———•••———

TRUST

So much is wrapped up in trust. Doesn't trust sometimes feel complicated?

"God, I believe you will heal me from this sickness."
"God, I really believe you will give me an 'A' on my boards."
"God, I know you will let our home sell by July 4th."
"God, I trust you'll let me win the Reader's Digest Sweepstakes, and I am even willing to tithe my $2 million prize."

What is the bedrock on which to build trust? Moses, the barefooted shepherd, hides his face as he stands before a burning bush. Out of the midst of the flame, a voice speaks:

> *"Listen. I am the God of your father...I have come down to deliver them. . . I will send you to Pharaoh..."* Exodus 3:6-12

Pressed with revelation, Moses says,

"If I am going to the Sons of Israel and I say the God of my father sent you, they may say, 'What is His name?' What shall I say?"

God's reply is a statement of truth as big as God Himself. It is truth that puts explosive force into every aspect of His character.

> *"God said to Moses, 'I Am who I Am.' And He said, 'Say this to the people of Israel: "I Am has sent me to you." ' "* Exodus 3:14

I Am

The words are cloaked in mystery. God desires us to know that His name means. . .

"He will be what He is."

First, it means that He is the ever-present one who stands outside of time. There is no past or future; everything is present. Our yesterdays as well as our tomorrows are all "now" to Him!

Secondly, this revelation name gives us the grace of God. **"I Am"** has no object. I am... what? He is saying, **"I am whatever My people need."** God is incomprehensible. But the moment human need or misery present themselves, He becomes just what the person needs. Do you lack peace? "I am that peace." Do you lack strength? "I am thy strength." Do you lack spiritual life? "I am thy life." Do you lack wisdom? "I am thy wisdom."

Just as water seeps to the lowest depths in order to fill the space, Yahweh is ever seeking out man's need in order to satisfy.

"Where there is need…there is God."

The **I Am** longs to turn your sorrow into blessings. Life is not the hungry seeking for bread but Bread seeking the hungry. It is not the sad one seeking joy but rather Joy seeking the sad one. It is not your empty being seeking fullness but rather the One that is full seeking to fill emptiness.

Imagine that you are a hospital patient awaiting surgery. You lie alone. Fear bursts to the surface. Your heart pounds. What will be the outcome? What will the pain be like?

Suddenly a neatly dressed man walks in carrying a black bag. Stepping closer to your bed and peering into your face, he asks,

"You are frightened, aren't you?"

"Oh yes! I really am. This is my first time in the hospital, and I am worried about how the surgery will come out in the morning."

"Listen to me," the man says. "I am here to tell you that you have nothing to worry about. You'll be fit as a fiddle."

Just about the moment you begin to relax from his words, the man walks over to the corner of the room, opens his black bag, and begins repairing the TV set.

"Right words…but wrong man!"

Later another neatly dressed man walks into your room. Coming closer to your bed, he looks down and says,

"You are frightened, aren't you?"

"Oh yes! I really am. This is my first time in the hospital, and I am worried about how the surgery will come out."

"Listen to me," the man says. "I am here to tell you that you have nothing to worry about. You'll be fit as a fiddle."

"And who are you?"

"I am the doctor who will be doing the surgery. I have checked with great care the X-rays and blood tests. I have gone over every detail. I have performed this surgery hundreds of times with no problems. You have nothing to fear. Trust me. . . everything will be all right."

The same words…but what a difference. What is the difference? **It is the character of the one who speaks that makes the difference!**

> *"For…I Am…Yahweh, who upholds your right hand, who says to you, 'Don't fear. I will help you.' "* Isaiah 41:13

> *"Can a mother forget her nursing child, and have no comparison on the son of her womb? Even these may forget, but I will not forget you. Behold, I have inscribed you on the palms of My hands."* Isaiah 49:15-16

Trust is resting…in the Faithfulness of the "I Am" to be who He says He is.

Trust in His name.

Jesus identifies that He is the **I Am**. His name, Je-sus, means, "I am thy salvation."

It is not what you trust…but whom. So Trust.

———•••———

HANDS

When God wanted to create the world, He merely had to use his…**fingers.**

> *"When I consider Your heavens, the work of Your fingers, the moon… the stars which You established."* Psalm 8:3

The finger of God shows the power of God creating and intervening in man's affairs. We see this with God's finger writing the Ten Commandments and in the New Testament (Luke 11:20) when Jesus refers to driving out demons by the "finger of God."

To save lost sinners He bore His…**arm.**

> *"Who has believed our message of that which*
> *Was revealed to us? And to whom has the arm*
> *of the Lord been disclosed."* Isaiah 53:1

His strong arms never tire, never let go…never allow adversity to pluck you away. These loving arms protect…fold…gently encourage. These encircling arms are greater than your little problems, and more massive than your overwhelming circumstances and more enduring than your "light affliction that is but for a moment."

"An eternal refuge…everlasting arms!"

With the coming changes in dentistry and medicine and the stresses and pressures of family life, isn't it great to know that your refuge is eternal? Be satisfied to rest in the full assurance that His **arms** will hold you.

When God wants to accomplish a task, He uses His mighty…**hand.**

"Ezra was a skilled scribe…and the king granted him all he asked for, the hand of the Lord his God was upon him." Ezra 7:6

The "hand" is viewed in the Old Testament as that part of the body that carries out a person's will. To give something into someone's hand is to give someone authority or to surrender it into his power. Symbolically, "hand" expresses strength, power, and especially God's power (Exodus 3:19-20) when it is used to perform His will.

"When God puts His children into the furnace, He keeps His **hand** on the thermostat and His eye on the thermometer."

In the New Testament the touching with "hands" is found 40 times, seen in connection with healings by Jesus. Isn't it always significant to see that Jesus touched people, and especially embraced and held children? Watch as children grab a hold of you, lean on you, and seek for your touch. Think of the times when your patients are facing death… the most appropriate thing is not to say anything but touch that person with your hand. The power of your love is transferred through those fingertips.

You may have money, or you may lose it all. You may have health, or it may leave you a dependent person. You may have friends, or you may find yourself very much alone.

Fingers… **arm**…**hand**…He reaches, He touches, He feels. In your loneliness, emphasized by sorrow of heart or bleak expectation of the future, God can give you a song in the night. The disciples with their feet fastened in the stocks and their backs bleeding from the beatings, were making melody in their hearts to the Lord.

"Thou will show me the path of life; at Thy right hand, there are pleasures forevermore." Psalm 16:11

Stand still long enough to allow God to put **His "hand"** on you and feel. As Eric Liddell said, "God made me fast. And when I run, I feel His pleasure."

Relax…fall into the hands of God. There you will find the eternal pleasures that you are striving for in the present. Remember, success is not based on who you are but "whose you are"!

—•••—

OMNI.SCIENCE

Do the days seem dark? Challenging politics…up and down economics…moral instability…sudden and anti-Christian changes in society.

"When you're in the dark…listen and God will give you a message to share with others when you get in the light." —Oswald Chambers

1 John 1:5 reveals

"God is light…in Him there is no darkness at all."

It seems so simple…light dispels darkness. God knows what is in the darkness.

"It is He who reveals the profound and hidden things. He knows what is…in the darkness and the light dwells within Him." Daniel 2:22

Nothing is hid from Him,
　　…escapes His "knowing,"
　　　　…is *ever* forgotten by Him.

God is omniscient—He knows everything that actually happens. He knows all possibilities of what could happen and what does not happen! He knows all events, creatures, and creation…all details. Nothing can be concealed from God.

"Neither the darkness of night nor the deepest dungeon can hide any from his eyes."
—A. W. Pink

God knows…God sees…we can't hide. Even though we often try. Adam and Eve hid in the trees of the Garden of Eden, after they sinned. They tried to "hide" from God and then "hurled" accusations at Him. God does not drive us like cattle, but he draws with the bonds and cords of love, so He says, "Adam, where are you?"

Not that He did not know where he was, but in order to appeal to Adam's mind, emotion, and will, He drew him out of hiding into the light…God's presence.

Sarah, who was barren in the womb, hearing an Angel saying she would be pregnant, laughed in the tent. God heard that and confronted her with it. She would not admit it. After Ai was defeated, Achan stole and hid gold from his fellow Israelites. God brought that into the light. King David tried to hide his affair with Bathsheba, but God brought it into the open. (So, how can we apply the omniscience of God to us as believers? How can we walk in the light?)

Comfort—God knows "the way that I take" (Job 23:10). He knows us intimately. He knows our frame. We are dust (Psalm 103:14). Jesus asked Peter, "Lovest thou Me?" Peter correctly replied, "Lord, thou **'knowest'** all things." He knows…He cares. We rest in knowing.

Prayer—This infinite knowledge of an infinite mind is capable of paying attention to millions at any one time. Prayer exposes our dependence, enables Him to respond, and lets us enjoy communing.

> *"Great is our Lord and abundant in strength. His understanding is inexhaustible and boundless."* Psalm 147:5

Amazement—Just as a mother hearing the cry of her child knows the needs, so our God, of infinite knowledge, lets me know that nothing we need escapes Him. So cry out!

"The eyes of the Lord in every place beholding evil and the good." Proverbs 15:3

Adoration—My past, present, future is present to Him. He has foreseen my every fault, every sin, every thought, and yet…He has fixed His heart upon me! Wonder and worship before Him!

The Lord God is Omni.scient.

———•••———

SURVIVAL OF THE UNFIT

Darwin's Theory contemplated "survival of the fittest and death to the unfit." Jesus' truth proclaims the opposite… since He is the fittest of all!

> *"You were redeemed with the precious blood of Christ, as a lamb without blemish and without spot."* 1 Peter 1:18-19

Christ died so that the unfit (we) might survive! Jesus' precious blood redeemed unfit people like you and me. He took death upon Himself so that our blemished sinful souls might not only survive but experience eternal life that begins here and now…will continue for all eternity.

As I walk with Jesus through the pages of scriptures, I see Him reaching out to the rejected, the blind, the lame, the dumb, the prostitute, the publicans; we see His compassion for those that were rejected by religious leaders as blemished lepers. Jesus even stopped a funeral procession to raise a dead son!

Consider we follow the lead of Jesus, the fittest of all, by placing our hearts and hands on those who are not surviving very well. I saw this in Philadelphia at the Summer Medical Institute as physicians and students went into the Latino area, the Bario. Judy and I had been there for six years.

But one particular year, I felt the trash on the streets, pain of the drug dealers, the prostitutes' cries, the broken families of young children raising themselves, no adults at home. I cried. As I cried, I thought, "Is it really true that God loves these individuals? God, are you crazy; do you really love the unlovely?" The answer: YES! For He has even loved me. Isn't it wonderful to recognize that we were unfit!

What a challenge to heal the body, repair teeth, even help those who can't see to see well. What a joy your profession is! But, also at the same time you meet physical needs, what a joy it is to seek out those viewing themselves as unfit, enable them to fall in love with Jesus, trusting Him as their Beloved.

People say, "Get a life!" Why don't you who has now been fitted out with the "clothes of Jesus' righteousness" allow Him to walk around in your body, think with your heart, and speak with your lips, to smile with your face, to touch with your hands?

Why don't we just be Jesus to those that God brings to us?

We don't need to go overseas or make a bigtime walk down the aisle; we just need to start being available.

"All that God is, is available to him who is available."

What an exchange! An unfit life exchanged for one who was totally acceptable to the Father.

— ••• —

WE HAVE

You have the best that life has to offer…when you have redemption. This present moment. If this is so, why not quit striving to gain what you already have?

"In Him we have redemption through His blood, remission of our offenses in accordance with the riches and generosity of His gracious favor." Ephesians 1:7

The above verse does not say you can work for it. Paul plainly states you have redemption when you have Jesus.

Swede Anderson, director of Latin America of Campus Crusade for Christ, had been in Mexico City training the staff with Campus Crusade. While there, Swede met a lady who had been supporting Campus Crusade for Christ in Mexico. This lady, who had never married, brought a man into her home to minister to him physically, having found him on the streets starving. Many of his normal "systems" were not working, and Swede, as he stood by the bed, found out the journey of his life.

When he was 6, his family had farmed him out to another family, giving them money to help pay his expenses. The adopted family took this child and chained him up, like an animal, in the back of their house. They took the money, using it for their own benefit. He was thrown scraps, no words of love were spoken, no ability to speak and learn languages was developed. Eventually, as a young man of 26, he was kicked out of that home and left to fend for himself on the streets.

That's when this lady saw him lying on the street malnourished, picked him up, brought him into her home, and bathed him, showing him love that he had never known. Swede, in the providence of God, shared with this man simply how he could make that wonderful discovery of knowing Jesus in a personal way. Though hardly able to speak in language he had never been taught…through tears in his eyes and the grasp of Swede's hand, he said, "I trust." Two weeks later when Swede came back to Mexico City to visit this man, he found out he had died. Just two weeks!

But, Swede realized, this man knew Jesus, unlike Winston Churchill, who had made such an impact in the world, had accolades of people and was so well educated and had the ability to communicate; to Swede's knowledge Winston had never trusted Jesus. In contrast to him, this man, upon trusting Christ, had it all…for you see, "In Him, we have redemption."

If this is true, why don't we live in light of our current possessions? This man had experienced forgiveness of his sins and extended forgiveness to those who had abused him. Why don't we accept this forgiveness? One possibility is we are so enfolded with "self-hatred."

Brennan Manning said, "If the Lord Jesus Christ has washed you in his own blood and forgiven you all your sins, how dare you refuse to forgive yourself?" Anything that causes division in the body of Christ is sinful. When you are divided within yourself, when you are so preoccupied with your own sins, egocentricity, and moral failures that you cannot hear the anguish cry of others, then you have suddenly re-established "self" as the center of focus and concern. Self-hatred is a sin. Biblically, that is idolatry.

"In Him we have redemption." Jesus has bought us out of the slave market of sin to be adopted as His daughter and son. Please join me in not acting like a beggar who claims to have no bread when fresh hot bread is rolling out of the person of Jesus Christ... the Bread of life to feed us. I have found I am good at forgiving others and not forgiving myself. Sounds humble, doesn't it? Actually, that's idolatry.

You do not need to go anywhere, do anything, give anything, love anything...just experience in this present moment all Jesus is since **you have redemption.**

•••

A GOOD NAME

"A good name is to be more desired than great riches; favor is better than silver and gold." Proverbs 22:1

A **good name,** once broken, may possibly be repaired, but the world will always keep their eyes on the spot where the crack was.

One important quality of life cannot be purchased with money: **a good name.** A name that is well spoken of is something we need to be careful to keep. Do you have a name that is associated with good things...right things...things of God? Once you develop a rotten name and your reputation is bankrupt, a million dollars cannot buy it back. To be poor is no disgrace; to have a questionable name is downright tragic.

Rare is the person who is fastened to the fix! These days people latch on to temporal sky hooks, grabbing hold of anything if it might swing a better deal. Like a swarm of fluttering butterflies, most people are flitting through life, seeking that which will satisfy their appetite.

If we have nothing beyond this perishable and material universe, it would indeed be misery to exist. Life would be not only insignificant but wretched, a meaningless, aimless ripple on the surface of the silent, shoreless sea.

Some people measure security by the length of their car, the size of their home, the depth of their practice; others, by the number of clubs, honors, organizations to which they belong. What is your measure of anchorage?

…Esau chose riches and thereby forgot his good name.
…Job chose a "good name" and thereby temporarily forfeited his fortune.
…Demas was careless with his name among good men and took off for Thessalonica, where he could gain material success and earthly security.

Alexander the Great was visiting his troops when he encountered an unshaved, rebellious, and drunken soldier.
"What is your name, soldier?"
"Alexander," replied the soldier.
"My man," commanded the emperor, "either change your conduct or change your name."

> *"And those who know your name put their trust in you, for you, O Lord, have not forsaken those who seek you."* Psalm 9:10

—•••—

BE STRONG, BE COURAGEOUS

> *"Be strong! Be courageous! Do not be afraid of them! For it is the Lord your God who goes with you. He will not fail you nor forsake you."* Deuteronomy 31:6

What is the antidote to fear? Is it to keep smiling…have a stiff upper lip…keep going…suck it in when everything is being pulled out?

Multitudes are haunted by the hazards of medical changes. Many are becoming panic-stricken from that which is real and that which is imaginary—they're scared to death of that which no one knows. They are fearful concerning the uncertain and unknown. Despairing is the person who feels the external. Panicked is the person who is haunted by the internal.

Fear is an enveloping fog that clouds a person's vision…like a cold, chilly hand upon the heart. "Be courageous" is our encouragement. The word "courage" comes from the Latin "cor" meaning "heart." The heart of a person is not to live with fear but with courage.

Fear sees the foe…Courage sees God! Gideon was a man of courage. He was a man so afraid of himself that he needed proof upon proof. . . but, he was so sure of God that he was confident they could rout the enemy with 300 men, a few trumpets to blow, and pitchers to smash.

"Afraid of himself…sure of God."

Courage is knowing your weaknesses…assured of God's divine presence.

What is the solution to fear? **FAITH!** Fear is the opposite of faith. Faith is believing that God is present. His promises are trustworthy. He has proven Himself in overcoming the fearing heart. Unbelief minimizes God by magnifying difficulties…fear.

In Mark 4:35-5:43, Jesus demonstrates His power over fear to His disciples. He puts them in circumstances to surface their fears and then demonstrates the solution. How? He demonstrates His authority or power over every realm in which he desires a faith-response. He rebuked the winds and waves of the storm. He taught them to respond with faith to "physical disaster." They arrived safely. A demon-possessed man confronts them on the shore. Jesus cast the legion of demons out, demonstrating His power over all "spiritual" things. After they go back to the opposite shore, Jesus shows how He has power over "physical disease." He demonstrated this when a woman who had hemorrhaged for twelve years touched Him. By resurrecting Jarius' twelve-year-old daughter, Jesus demonstrated His power over all "supernatural" things, even death. He has power or authority over all—disasters…demons…disease…and death.

> *"I sought the Lord…and He heard me and delivered me from all my fears."* Psalm 34:4

The remarkable thing about fearing God is… **When you fear God you fear nothing else.** If you don't fear God **you fear everything else.** As we rush out into the future let us go by faith, not by fear. **Be strong! Be courageous! He has the power!**

TASTE AND SEE

The God we worship is a most mysterious God. **Incomprehensible!** He refuses to be impressed with our neat theological boxes as though we could make a list of statements about Him, draw a circle around Him, and say "Aha! We've got it." Not only are God's thoughts not our thoughts nor our ways His ways, but Paul even said to the Corinthians that the "Foolishness of God is wiser than man's wisdom." **God will always be greater than our greatest thought.** Explain His love or patience and power and wisdom? He wants us to know that we can't know all there is to know.

"Oh, taste and see...that the Lord is good." Psalm 34:8

How do you define a Georgia peach? Well, you could say it is about 3 or 4 inches in diameter, and it is oval. Fuzzy outside and big seed in the middle. Multicolored with reddish and yellow skin. Sweet juicy taste. Very unmistakable fragrance. Isn't it so much more joyful to either bite in or peel and eat with ice cream in the lazy days of summer? Did I just define a peach? Not really. Some could give a chemical analysis. Others could give a spectroscopic definition of its color densities. Would that do it? No! A peach must be experienced.

This is precisely what the Bible says about our relationship with God. How does one go about "tasting" God? **Nurturing love takes time.** It doesn't simply happen. If you take time for daily Bible reading and prayer, you need to stop and meditate on what you have read. Slow down long enough to talk to God...about God. "To taste Him" would be to enjoy the sheer pleasure of His love and forgiveness. Tasting Him will come only after those heavy, hurting struggles up the steep sides of an obstacle that seem to make no sense at all. Finally at the top, if we are not careful, we will slide down the far side with a sigh of relief without first pausing to drink in the view from the top.

I once went to a retreat outside of Baton Rouge, Louisiana, to be with a group of people who were involved in our ministry at LSU. From Jackson, Mississippi, we took the Natchez Trace. I was in such a hurry to get to our location that I missed all the spots along the way that had historical significance. I then got tired and took a nap, missing all the beauty of the drive through the area. Upon arrival at the retreat those who had suggested the route were greatly disappointed to hear I had only noticed the sign saying "Leaving Natchez Trace." I had been through it...but had not really tasted it!

Let's not do that with Jesus. Let's stop along the way, inhale and reflect, smell the flowers, and see the weeds.

Pause long enough…to see and…to taste…the Lord is Good!

— ••• —

LIKE A CHILD

"Truly I say to you unless you are converted and become like children…you shall not enter the Kingdom of heaven." Matthew 18:2

Are you a child? What is a childlike attitude? A child's attitude is one of listening to the voice of the father and seeking to act upon the father's desires.

"Speak, Lord, for thy servant is listening." I Samuel 3:10

If you are occupied with many good things but not the best, you do not hear God in comments, whispers, breezes through the trees, or other servants of God. When the Israelites come out of Egypt, God used a cloud to simplify their belief until their relationship with Him was that of a child. The only vision and direction came from God; other people faded into the shadows.

What are some of the characteristics of a child?

Children are wonder-filled about life's objects. They are intense in their focus of investigation, confident in the security of the family. At the same time, they live in helplessness and dependence. **So…be dependent on Jesus!**

Their lives are characterized by simplicity, hope, awkwardness, and affection. Do your children put their hands all over you? I observe children in church as they hug, touch, stroke, and look for strokes. Do you want someone to touch you? **Jesus can!**

Children trust their fathers. Isaac, the son of Abraham, showed he trusted his father by carrying the wood for his own sacrifice to the top of the mountain. Can you imagine the pain of Abraham as he saw his son walking up with an expectation of the sacrifice, but also the joy of an expectant resurrection? Isaac trusted the father. **They came down…together!**

What kind of father did you have? Loleeta, our former secretary, said she had a wonderful father. She trusted him and would argue with friends, saying, "My Daddy can do this or build that. . . he can do anything."

Fathers want us to submit in order for them to meet our needs. Jesus said, ***"Before Abraham was, I AM"*** (John 8:58). What does that mean? It is an unfinished sentence; it has no object. I AM – what? He is saying, "**I AM…**whatever my people need." This sentence is left blank so a child may complete it with as many needs as arise.

The moment human need and misery present themselves, He becomes just what that child needs. Do we lack peace? I am…your peace. Do we lack strength? I am…your strength. Do we lack spiritual life? I am…your life. Do we lack wisdom? I am…your wisdom.

Fathers enjoy meeting needs. Just as water is ever seeking the lowest depths in order to fill them, so God, as our Father, is ever seeking out his children's needs…in order to satisfy them.

"Where there is need…there is God."

The "I AM" yearns to turn man's sorrow into trust. It is not, therefore, the hungry seeking for bread but the Bread seeking the hungry; not the sad seeking for joy but rather Joy seeking the sad; not emptiness seeking fullness but Fullness seeking emptiness. He is the ever-present "I AM"…children need.

Patient loads go up, fear of the future, anxiety in the present, guilt in the past…none of these are to be the providence of a child. **Why not choose to become like a child?**

Are you self-sufficient, or are you becoming…like a child?

———•••———

FURIOUS TENDER LOVE

Life's motivation will become life's master.

To define love is wonderful, but to experience it is even greater! Jewish men were not allowed to read the Song of Solomon until after age 19 or prior to the consummation of the marriage relationship. The amazing intricacies, the beauty, the challenge, and nourishment of marital love is so aptly described in Song of Solomon 8:5-7.

"Who is this coming up from the wilderness, leaning on her Beloved?" (v. 5)

By analogy God's love is described through use of illustrations that love **is painful... possessive...persevering...priceless...and protective.**

"There your mother was in labor with you, there she was in labor and gave you birth." (v. 5)

God's love is painful. This is shown in the analogy of a mother in child-labor. Just this week as I came to pray with a physician's wife in labor prior to getting her epidural, I saw the pain and tears that came out of the edge of her eye, crying out, "How can this be so painful?" Then I later heard of the great joy the couple experienced as a little girl was placed upon her mother's breast for her to nurture. God's love is like that! The love of the child is greater than the pain in giving birth.

It was mere minutes till the crushing agony of Gethsemane. Scarce hours before the horror of the cross when Jesus said...

"But that the world will know that I love the Father and as the Father gave me the commandment, even so I do. Arise, let us go up from here." John 14:31

Go where?

To the cross, to unspeakable torture, to pain...loneliness...humiliation...suffering beyond conception.

Often, we are told that the cross reveals how much God loves us, and that is true. But the cross also reveals **how much Jesus loved His Father.** Every act of obedience to His Father was an affirmation of His love. Can't you just imagine you are hearing faint whispers in the stinging lashes of scourging, "I love you...Abba."

A mother lays down her life for her child. Nothing is advertised of her sacrifice. The child will never recognize what the mother has done until the child herself is in the same place; then she will recognize the unadvertised substitution of the mother's life and... love. This is what Jesus has done. "He laid down His life for us." Jesus expects us to be made broken bread and poured-out wine in His hands...for others. If we are not thoroughly baked, we will produce indigestion...because we are dough instead of bread.

God's love is Possessive...as described in Song of Solomon 8:

"For love is as strong as death, Jealousy is as severe as Sheol. Its flashes are flashes of fire, the flame of the Lord." (v. 6)

Having been around physicians who treated patients long days and nights and then they die, I've found they uniquely feel the force of death. The finality of it. A neonatologist said the hardest part of his job was to tell the parents their child died. Painful. God's love is so possessive that it is as certain and it is as strong as death. God's possessive love can best be described as a "jealous love" that would be as severe as death. God has not pursued you in order that you might be betrothed to another. The intensity of the feeling that you have toward your spouse shows the intensity of your love. If inside, you could say you couldn't care less what they do, you actually care less for them.

God's love is not only possessive but also persevering.

"Many waters cannot quench love, nor will rivers overflow it." (v. 7)

The strength of the river comes as the walls of the mountain press in, producing white water. The power and the persevering of the water flowing downstream shows how persevering God's love is for each of us. It cannot be stopped! Ride with the flow!

God's love is not only persevering but also priceless. Solomon said,

"If a man were to give all the riches of his house for love, it would be utterly despised." (v. 7)

There is no measure to measure the value of God's love for us. The worth of something is determined by what someone is willing to pay for it. **What was God willing to pay for you?** His Son...His only Son? You are worth infinite value! Why not enjoy this? Why not treat yourself...as God treats you?

I love you. Under the pressure of the crown of thorns, Jesus said, "I love you...Father. I love you." As the nails pierced through his flesh..."I love you...I...love...you."

Put me...like a seal over your heart...like a seal on your arm. (v. 6a)

Not only are we birthed in pain of God's love, but **His love is protective.** The bride of Solomon asked for a "seal" over the heart—the seat of affections—and "seal" over the arm—the seat of power for protection. The King used his signet ring to protect the documents he sent. Jesus' tomb was sealed and guarded. Why not be secure...in His love?

"If you can't trace His plan,
    If you can't see His hand,
        Trust His heart."

Think of the parent during a child's day by day, moment by moment, watchful protection. "Don't run in the street!" God is so protective, He says that there will be nothing beyond what we will be able to withstand. Sometimes I do not feel this way, but it is truth.

"We know love...by this, that He laid down His life...for us; and we ought to lay down our lives for the brethren." 1 John 3:16

Our Response? Ten leprous men were healed by Jesus. Of the ten, only one, when he discovered that he was healed, returned to Jesus to give him thanks and to glorify God. The other nine went on their way eager to enjoy their new life that the healing had provided.

To them, the Lord Jesus was but the **"means to an end,"** the end being a life of health. But the one who fell down at His feet, craving fellowship with the One who had healed him, Jesus was not only the **"means" but the "end" Himself.** Jesus is not a means to an end. Our end...is to be like the Lord Jesus...Himself.

The reason that we are to stay in fellowship, have revival or power with God, to be used by Him or have this or that blessing, is not for this but **that we might have Him. Either He will be "the end" of all of our lives or "idols" will take His place in our hearts.** Respond!

"What you bend your knee to...is what you worship."

Life's motivation...will become...life's master.

———•••———

SPEAKING THE TRUTH IN LOVE

What role does your love play in the growth of another individual?

"Do I love you because you are beautiful...or are you beautiful because I love you?"

Does your love contribute to someone's beauty? Can your care and compassion alter their character? If I love you, can you become more lovable?

Marriage is like a garden in which one person plants the seed of their life in the soil of another's life. God has planted us in the soil of His perfect love. *"That you, being rooted and grounded in love..."* Colossians 3:17. To whom are you a soil? Do you have the ingredients of a healthy growth-producing soil? What are the critical elements that stunt the growth of another individual? Love is the soil (context). Truth is a seed (content). When truth is communicated by a love-flavored person, growth is the expected result.

> **"Speaking the truth in love, we will grow up into all things in Him."**
> Ephesians 4:15

Note the three key elements: the **truth**...in **love**...will **grow.**

This spring I had to "speak the truth" to a friend who has meant so much to me. My advice was painful. Did I speak...in love? I was reprimanded by this dear friend. He spoke the truth, as he knew it...but he was angry. This was painful. How can we hear truth if we don't hear love?

Truth. Truth is the basic stuff of growth. Are you open to the truth...about yourself? A truly lovable person refuses to run from facts. They welcome them, painful as they may be at times. As God's agents for truth, we are to intercept the lives of others in such a way that truth impacts and changes their lives. But, that doesn't mean that we can communicate the truth in any old way we please. It must be communicated "in love."

"Truth without love is brutality."

Effective communication is the blending of the proper content (truth) with the proper context (love).

Love. Love is the soil for truth to be built in. If your purpose is to cause growth, not winning or proving your point, you'll make sure the truth you know is communicated in love. The discipline of a child works because he has disappointed someone who loves him. Discipline outside the context of love usually produces resentment and bitterness. It is a delicate relationship between the acceptance of truth and the assurance of love. **It's not what is said that creates a problem, but how it is said.** If I sense you really care, that you're committed to my growth, I not only love the truth but also am likely to respond to it—learn from it. A lovable person checks the context for love, proceeding if he gets yes to these questions:

1) Do I really care?   2) Is it true?   3) Will it help?

Growth. All things grow up. How can you really love another if you're unconcerned about that individual's growth? The intent of every true love uses every resource at their command to stimulate growth. How will your responses to your husband, wife, child, or friend be different if their growth is your number one concern? Ask yourself this question: "Will what I'm about to say or do contribute to this person's growth?" If it won't, don't say it or do it. Lovable people apply "growth checks" before they react or respond.

The seed is truth...the soil is love...the proper relationship between them produces growth. If the soil isn't right, truth isn't going to produce much fruit. **Love is the filter for all truth.**

I trust that you have someone **speaking the truth...in love...so that in all things you will grow in Christ.**

———•••———

BOTTOM LINE

The older I get, the simpler I want "it." When it comes down to the Bottom Line it's...

"Love" (Agape)

Judy and I have just gone through another year of seeing students graduate from medical school. We have helped pack trucks, care for children, and send food and have had some who spent their last night at our home before heading to their residency. It has been hard. Why? Some of these we have been involved with for four years. We knew them when they were single or young marrieds and prayed for them to get pregnant. We prayed all during their pregnancy. We arrived at the hospital before the delivery. I had the opportunity to pray blessings upon the newborn child and then each Monday night I held many of them as we were preparing food, eating, and having the support group each week. It hurts to see those you have loved leave. But the greater the capacity we have for hurt, the greater capacity we have for love. For as I have often quoted:

"To have been hurt much, indicates that you loved much."

Judy and I have enjoyed being substitute parents and adopting so many of their children as our grandchildren. Even though we experience this human love, it will always be a faint shadow of God's love...and a thin echo of His passion.

Love needs an object. What if that object does not appear to be worthy of love?

"If anyone says 'I love God' and detests or hates his brother in Christ, he's a liar; for he who does not love his brother whom he has seen, cannot love God whom he has not seen." 1 John 4:20

Perfect love consists of being able to find a person lovable in spite of his or her weaknesses…faults…and imperfections. A person's assertion that they love the invisible when it appears that they do not love the visible is not love. The more you love the unseen, the more you will love the people you see. In imparting to these couples the importance of loving the people we "see," I said to them, "Watch your 'should be.'" It is important that we do not imagine how we wish they "should be." Those who allow themselves to do this do not love the person they see but something unseen, such as their own ideas.

In pre-marriage counseling I see individuals attracted to those who are opposite to themselves. After marriage, they seek to change that individual to fit their own desires. Rejection, not acceptance, is set up, and thus begins the battleground. The motives are often very good; we wish it not merely for our own sake but for their benefit as well. However, we are to love our spouse with their weaknesses. The weaknesses of your lover do not necessarily make you a stranger to each other. It should make your relationship come closer, more inwardly together in order to overcome the weaknesses. This shows precisely that you love your spouse in whom you "see" the fault or weakness or imperfection.

God's love for us is limitless. It is based on prior knowledge: He knew us even before we were created. How do you see your spouse, your children…is your love limitless? Is your love available to give them the freedom to change, according to God's will?

When it comes down to "it," it's limitless, unmerited love seen…felt…touched because of Jesus.

—•••—

THE TRUTH

"Rather, speaking the truth in love. We are to grow up…"
Ephesians 4:15

Jesus is not saying when He says, "I am the truth" that He merely teaches us the truth, as if the truth were something apart from Himself. But that He, Himself, is the Truth. To see Him, is to see true Truth.

Where do we see Jesus as the Truth? Supremely on the cross. There, in Him, we see the whole naked truth about us…sin…and God. This scene reveals the richest and sweetest grace of God toward us as it also reveals the starkest truth as to what man is. If Grace flows from the cross, so does Truth, for both ***"grace and truth came by Jesus Christ."*** (John 1:17)

Truth is a person.

Not a system or creed. Jesus Christ, himself, is the truth about the Father's desired relationship with us. Looking at the face of Jesus Christ, marred and scared for us, we see God is not against the sinner but for him; he's not our enemy but our friend, offering peace, forgiveness, new life. The cross of Christ has been called "the surprising generosity of Christ." It not only surprises our guilty conscience but also melts, draws, and causes us to run to him with honesty, knowing that nothing…nothing but mercy is waiting for us.

What is our response to this revelation of Truth?

> ***"For everyone who does evil hates the light, and does not come to the light, lest his deeds should be exposed. But he who practices the truth comes to the light, that his deeds may be manifested as having been wrought in God."*** John 3:20,21

It doesn't say "he who does good," but "he who practices the Truth"

…so practice Truth! What God asks, first of all, is plain truthful repentance, based on the cross of Jesus. For pardon, forgiveness…then with truth we experience the peace of God. How many medications can you prescribe for the patient to gain peace?

Are you needy? Truth can become of vital interest to you, when you are between the Rock and the hard place. Seek Truth in the person of Jesus. Rest…relax, for Jesus is the Word made flesh. Jesus is Truth with skin on. Crawl into His lap and allow his arms to enfold His most precious possession…you!

How do we apply **"Speaking the Truth"** with spouse, friends, colleagues, patients, and enemies? Note there is a balance. It is not just "speaking with truth," which could be like a naked scalpel, or is it just dealing with someone "in love" and ignoring their responsibility?

Salt heals. The healing of salt occurs because of the combination of sodium plus chloride. Each of these in their separateness could hurt, corrode, and not achieve a desired result. Combined together, and applied in a diagnostic situation, those elements in unity will perform its purpose. Just so, it is to **"speak the truth…in love."**

Are you in a situation now where you see "truth" but you are not speaking in "love," or are you seeking to be "loving," yet not being honest to share truth? Keep the balance. You will do as Jesus has done for you. The balance has now gained eternal life! Be salt!

Keep speaking the truth…in love.

— ••• —

THE IN.NESS

Christ **"*in*"** you makes you fit to live on the earth. You **"*in*"** Christ makes you fit for heaven!

"Strengthen with His might by His Spirit **'*in*'** the *inner* man."

"That Christ may dwell **'*in*'** your hearts."

"Rooted and grounded **'*in love*'** according to the power that works in us."

"Christ **'*in*'** you, your only hope of glory."

Amazing. Christ **_in_** me is my only hope of glory! Think about it. Not my practice, not my family, not my success.

"A Christian is not a person on earth looking up to heaven, but a person in heaven looking down on earth."

The Christian life is not the Christian imitating Christ but is Christ actually **_in_** the life…imitating Himself. The perfect copy of Christ's life can be reproduced only by Christ Himself. We need the Copier to write the copy! We need the Blesser for the blessing, the loving Christ for the compassionate heart, the Graced One for the graciousness of Christ, the peace of Christ by the Prince of Peace, the faith of Christ for us to live by faith.

Christ is independent of all, but all of us are dependent upon Him. The measure of God's working through us is limited and gauged by His working **in** us.

> **"Now unto Him, who is able to do exceedingly abundantly above all we ask or think according to the power that works 'in' us."**
> Ephesians 3:19,20

The key phrase above is "according to" (*kata* in Greek), which means "under the dominion of." Kata suggests an object bending toward another in order to meet its need. The human side of your prayer life is met by the divine side of God's ability and working. We ask much, think more, but He does more and thinks greater.

The privilege of prayer is found in "ask," the in-ness of prayer is suggested by "think," and the supply of prayer is discovered "abundantly." The encouragement of prayer is revealed in "God is able," His sufficiency. His work means displacement of self and the enthronement of Christ.

To be "in Christ" is to be in the place of reality, for Christ is reality

…Truth is a person.

All fakeness, falsehood, and pretense die, and the real person emerges "in Christ." For to be "in Christ" is to be "in Christ" in the world!

Will you open the door to let Him come in? *In* Christ, will you let Him live by the power of the Holy Spirit, the supernatural Christian life? Will you allow Him to be available? He's capable!

The Christian life is not difficult to live…it's impossible…unless Christ lives it. Step aside and let Him think with your mind, love with your heart, speak with your lips… relish…rest…you're *in* Christ!

———•••———

THE VALLEY OF BACA

"Passing through the valley of Baca, they make it a spring. The early rain also covers it with blessings." Psalm 84:6

The valley of tears is called **Baca,** or **"weeping,"** which is the last stage of the pilgrimage from North Palestine to Jerusalem. This narrow valley has water trickling out of rocks, which makes it appear the rocks have many years on them. Also, the balsam trees exuded a gum used for medical purposes to heal wounds and to cure stomach troubles. Is this why it was said Jesus is the balm of Gilead, the Great Prescriber, the Great Physician?

A valley is defined in the dictionary as "a depression" or a very steep-sided valley (i.e., gorge) that came about from streams cutting out the limestone and sandstone.

Isn't it interesting that valleys are called "a depression"? Where does depression come from? Sometimes it feels like a dry, barren wind off a lonely desert. And something inside us begins to wilt. At other times it feels like a chilling mist. Seeping through our pores it numbs the spirit and fogs the path before us.

"You cannot have a mountain without a valley."

Valleys we go through are not by chance but are by purpose to surface imperfections and more importantly to eliminate them. The effects of winter present a lively image of God's purpose. As the season of cold approaches, the trees gradually lose their leaves going from vivid greenness into browns and golds…which then fall and die. The trees now look stripped and dead; the loss of their summer garments brings to light all the surface defects that previously had been hidden from view.

As for us, our trials strip us of our protective leaves. What is the effect of winter? It redirects the sap in the winter from being expended outwardly and concentrates its strength upon new roots and forcing old ones deeper into the soil of God's marvelous love. You may feel "dead" but you have never been healthier and more alive as during the winter of this compression set. **Are you sure of this?**

God uses the winter seasons of our lives not to give new defects but to uncover the old ones so that they would be openly exposed…so they may be better healed.

Jesus sitting in the garden of Gethsemane saw the winter of His life not for His defects but for the defects of you and…especially me. It was said of Jesus upon the cross "His heart was like wax." It melted in the midst of His receiving our sins. Isn't it amazing a Savior of inestimable value was cast into the gross sea of our sins? He dissolved them, allowing those to be replaced by His immeasurable acceptance and grace.

Jesus' love is stronger than death. It can touch the heart and melt it more quickly than any other power.

Where are you in the "winter of discontent"? Are you in the "valley of weeping" looking up at the mountain and wondering if you could ever reach that peak? Are you looking for a shelter and a refuge? David found it.

> *"Turn your ear to me! Come quickly to my rescue! Be my rock of refuge and a strong fortress to save me."* Psalm 31:2

David's refuge never failed. Not even once. Even in the valley of Baca…he never regretted the times that he dropped his heavy load and ran for cover.

Neither will you.

———•••———

GOSSIP

"He who answers a matter before he hears the facts, it is folly and shame to him." Proverbs 18:13

Is passing judgment upon another ever the duty of a Christian?

Never—if before hearing the facts of the case, you come up with a verbal verdict. This is prejudice. Proverbs says "folly and shame" are going to be your rewards.

What about the juicy news that you think only you know about? Hold it. Swallow it. Do not allow it to pass through your lips.

"In a multitude of words, transgression is not lacking, but he who restrains his lips is prudent." Proverbs 10:19

In many cases…silence is golden!

Believers should not speak evil of others, because they are different from others. Those who speak evil of others have a good opinion of themselves. They take the blackness of others as a dark background to bring out the whiteness and supposed greater prominence of their own virtues.

Believers who have the nature of the Spirit should feed upon the grain of truth, not the grain of old flesh vultures. If we are aware of evil, we can seek to remove it by rescuing those who are in its power. If you speak about any sin you see in others, you are showing a lack of love in your own heart, for "love covers a multitude of sins."

Speaking evil ignores the distinct command of the Lord not to speak evil of others (James 4:11). A church member was speaking unkindly of a missionary and was asked, "Is she a Christian?" "Yes, I think she is" was the reply. "Well, since Jesus loves her in spite of all of her faults, why is it you can't?" The way to kill the evil…of evil speaking…is to look at others with the eyes of Jesus, see how He regards them, and then follow His example.

To speak evil of others is to bring evil upon ourselves, or at least to keep blessing from us. Hasty conclusions and a biased spirit reveal a warped, twisted, and superficial heart. "Out of the abundance of the heart, the mouth speaks." The "fleshly mind" is in no position to act as the critic, for it is harsh…intolerant…and loves to cut to pieces the life of another. They believe, "If I can cut him down to size, it will tend to lift me up!"

Give yourself this little three-way test before you speak about someone: **Is it kind? Is it necessary? Is it true?**

> *"Set a guard, O Lord, over my mouth;*
> *keep watch over the door of my lips!"* Psalm 141:3

Let us pray that the Lord will cleanse our hearts…clear our vision…and then we shall have clear tongues.

— ••• —

FOCUS

We become like what we focus on.

> *"Like newborn babes, long for the milk of the word, that by it you may grow in respect of salvation."* 1 Peter 2:2

It is a scientific fact in the animal kingdom that insects become like the thing on which they feed; for instance, caterpillars, feeding upon a certain vegetable, become so like it that they can scarcely be distinguished from the plant on which they are found.

The same thing is true with regard to our spiritual life. The striking instance of this is the Old Testament experience of Josiah in 2 Kings 23:3-25. The direct effects of his reading the Word of God resulted in the putting away of all idolatrous practices and everyone's endeavor to perform the words that were written.

Isn't it so true "the word of God will keep you from sin or sin will keep you from the word of God"?

Christ says, *"The words that I speak to you, they are spirit, and life"* (John 6:63). The all-producing fact embodied in these words is, we cannot have the spirit nor His life apart from His word. The flow of God's word and the living flame in it are so tied into one that the Holy Spirit cannot be had apart from God's word any more than the plant can be apart from the seed producing it.

All that the plant will ever be is latent in the seed. The color, style, height, length, depth, and the breath all are determined by the characteristic of the seed. So it is with the word of God.

When the Word is received into the soil of our hearts, it manifests itself in a consecrated life.

To make obvious what was hidden in the seed it must be placed in a suitable environment. Seeds found in tombs in Egypt, placed under necessary conditions, begin to grow. The seed and the Word of God must be sewn in the soil of faith. It will only develop in the ground on obedience. **When the word of God's grace is joined in the faith of our obedience then there will be evidence of His Life.** As we submit to the direction of the word, it will transmit the beauty of its life.

If you will feed upon the Word, you will indeed become like it. The Word of God does not give up its secrets nor its nourishment to the casual or careless reader. If you were to gaze upon an artwork such as Michelangelo's at the Sistine Chapel, you might be disappointed at first glance; however, if you look at it again and again (focus), with more depth you would see the brilliant design and workmanship. This is also true for those who ponder the Word of God.

Let us ponder the Word of God…prayerfully, live it out carefully, practice it thoroughly, abide in it constantly, and believe in it wholly.

Then our lives will be aglow with love. Labor for Christ will be a lightsome task. **We become like what we focus on.**

Stay focused!

———•••———

TWO PEOPLE—TWO WAYS—TWO DESTINIES

Which way have you decided to walk? Psalm 1 says there are only two ways: God's way and man's way. This passage's main principle is…

"Whatever shapes a man's thinking…shapes his life."

Decision determines direction, and direction determines destiny.

Psalm 1, being a sketch of the other 149, is the resume of a truly happy (blessed) person. The rest of the book tells us how to live and enjoy this unique life of overflow. It contrasts what the happy person does not do with the one thing he does do, which is to delight in the law of the Lord. Is God's delight your delight? Note the contrast between the godly who does one thing and the other person who is like chaff—fruitless, weightless, rootless, useless.

"Prayer is a golden river at whose bank some die of thirst…

while others kneel and drink."

The righteous are like a tree…the wicked are like chaff. One has a solid foundation; the other is swept away by folly.

The contrast is sharp and in focus. The choice is inevitable. We must all make it. Which person will you be known as?

Be known by the company you avoid! This is negative purity, but it is a pathway you must follow. There are definite prohibitions: "Walk not…stand not…sit not." These are absolute statements of unchanging laws of spiritual declension.

"It is a sign of inward grace when the outward walk is changed."

Be known by the things you love! This is the love of positive pursuits. Here is a person who gets excited about Holy Scriptures and does not consider them a drag or a bore but can say, "How sweet are their words to my taste; yea, sweeter than honey to my mouth!" This is the around-the-clock Christian who meditates morning, afternoon, and night.

Be known by what you are. A person can hate sin and love righteousness when he is grounded and fixed in the soil of God's marvelous love. This person can do something because they are something. They can bear fruit because they have a "root" system. They do not run out of gas because they are always in reach of an unfailing supply.

Where do you get your input? If you get your input from the Word, it will give your **mind** godly assumptions and perspectives. These will produce an **attitude** of Spirit-filled idealism and optimism, which will **result** in the action of trusting and walking by faith. This victorious life can be explained only by God. Are you allowing Satan and the world to fill your **mind** with worldly assumptions and perspectives? This produces an **attitude** of worldly realism and **results** in action of walking by sight and dictates a life of pessimism, disillusion, and defeat.

Wouldn't you rather be like a tree that is planted by streams of living water that is prosperous, perennially young, vigorous, and fresh…and has a guarantee of permanence? "Its leaf does not wither."

As my daddy used to say, "You can't run with the rabbits and hunt with the hounds... you must choose!"

Be known by the company you avoid, the things you love, and what you are. **Don't fade coming down the home stretch of life...be like a tree!**

———•••———

HIS GLORY AND OUR GOOD

"Then his wife said to him, 'Do you still hold fast to your integrity? Curse God and die!' But he said to her, 'You speak as one of the foolish women speak. Shall we indeed accept good from God and not accept adversity?' In all this, Job did not sin with his lips." Job 2:9-10

Do you seem to be up against a brick wall with no visible way through? All is black... bleak...and uncertain! At the moment you take a single step in faith, wham...the way is opened.

Has God been a God of silence or a God of the eleventh hour? Timely...is often His way of meeting our every need at the right moment! "God may not be early, but He is never late!"

Providence "is God's way of allowing us to stand upon the brink of a precipice and then in the nick of time when another step and you would fall over, He stretches out His mighty arm to save."

The two-fold objective of God's Providence:
>—His own glory
>>—the good of His people

God never pursues His glory at the expense of the good of His people, nor does He ever seek our good at the expense of His glory. He has designed His eternal purpose so that His glory and our good are intricately bound together.

Can you trust God? You can if God is trustworthy.

The next question is, Can God always care for us? Is He in control (is He sovereign), and does He always care for us (is He good)? God's Providence affirms that we can trust

God since He does care for us…constantly.

We see the beginning…or the middle…just a small fragment of life. God sees and plans the beginning from the end. Life is not a gamble. Circumstances and events in your daily life are as threads in the tapestry of your life that the Lord God is the weaver. His purposes for our life flow like an irresistible current of the ocean.

Nothing is too big to evade His grasp. How do we know? Well, if His eye is on the fallowing sparrow, how much more He knows the perils of your daily walk—the wrongs that you suffer, the ill treatment that is dispensed, the heartaches and the loneliness through which you often pass. There is no detail so minute as to escape His interest. Be mighty thankful that in His Providence you don't get all that you ask for; shortsightedness fails to see the end.

The Providence of God is seen so clearly in the life of Joseph. Joseph is sold into slavery by His brothers, who live with this guilt for the next twelve years. While in Egypt, Joseph became very successful. God caused a famine; He also provided a way for dealing with it, for He already had Joseph in Egypt in a position of authority.

All people—believers as well as unbelievers—experience anxiety, frustrations, heartache, and disappointment. Some suffer intense physical pain and tragedy, but that which distinguishes the suffering of believers from unbelievers is the confidence that our suffering is under the control of an all-powerful, all-loving God. Our suffering has meaning and purpose in God's eternal plan, and He brings or allows to come into our lives only that which is for His glory…and our good.

Paul says we can entrust our most valuable possessions to the Lord.

> *"That is why I am suffering as I am, yet I am not ashamed, because I know whom I have believed, and am convinced that He is able to guard what I've entrusted to Him until that day."* 2 Timothy 1:12

Accept adversity for His glory and your good.

— •••—

LITTLE THINGS

Little things…mean a lot. Haven't you found this to be true with your patients and your family? The touch of a hand, a word said, a sacrifice made…a smile given.

"Four things are small on the earth, but they are exceedingly wise."
Proverbs 30:24

Greatness in life is often found in miniature. The weak…the little…the insignificant can teach us lessons completely unknown to the elephant, the lion, the Olympiad greats. Solomon wisely illustrates the truth—to be little does not mean you are nothing—using four insects as examples.

"The ants are not strong, but they prepare their food in summer" (v. 25). Ants have a built-in sense of doing the right thing at the right time. They know there will come a time when they can't do what they need to do. This is the purpose of prayer. You need to pray now, for you will need it later. Pray for your children's mate now, protection for your spouse. From the small ant we can learn the lesson of provision.

"The badgers are not mighty folk, yet they make their houses in the rocks" (v. 26). The badgers have an uncanny instinct of where to live. Feebleness forces him to well-guarded fortifications. Because he realizes his weakness and lack of strength, he chooses to live in the rocks. Do you know your strengths? Your weaknesses? Your shortcomings? If you do, you can be wise and flee to "The Rock." Look at *Psalm 91:1-2. From the wise badgers we can learn the lesson of protected shelter.*

"The locusts have no king, yet all of them go out in ranks" (v. 27). Locusts do not have a leader, but they keep together…in one accord to get the job done. When they move they move like a mighty army…in mass, fused as one body. In the body of Christ, we are all a part of the unified body with one Head, Christ. Are you in the body of Christ or breaking rank? Thank your spouse for making you be so effective. From the band of locusts, we can learn the lesson of partnership.

"The lizard you may grasp with the hands, yet it is in the king's palaces" (v. 28). Insignificant, yet they end up in the king's palace. Everyone is against them, daily attempting to destroy them. Yet they keep on keeping on! There are no insignificant places for you to be involved in your medical ministry when you are serving our wonderful Lord Jesus Christ. From the lizard you can learn the lesson of persistence.

Greatness is often in miniature. There are no small people, only small ideas. Some people impress us with powerful personal images. In others, we see weakness, whether in health or character. But only God can see deep into a person's being to determine whether they are strong or weak.

God can accomplish His purposes in us as we subordinate our own efforts to His power. Our ultimate dependence is only upon God...all other dependence is temporal.

Yes, these four things (provision, protected shelter, partnership, and persistence) are small, but they are exceedingly wise and only get larger in our lives as we apply them in little increments to our character.

Little things truly mean a lot!

—•••—

IN YOUR FACE!

There is no spot where God is not. **He is omnipresent.**

God's friend Moses wanted to see the Glory of God.

> ***"And the Lord said, 'I will cause all my goodness in front of you. I will proclaim my Name, the Lord, in your presence but you can not see my face...for no one may see me and live.'"*** Exodus 33:18

Wherever you are at this moment, God is there...in all of His majestic fullness. . . in His radiant splendor.

When God speaks of His presence, He is speaking of ***"His face."*** Moses said,

> *"If Thy 'presence' does not go with us, do not lead us up from here."*

Moses knew that not only is God here but He is always aware of you! Have you ever been in a crowded elevator but you felt terribly alone? There you are in silence, shoulder to shoulder with a dozen people, and everyone watching the floor numbers. It is as though "you" don't matter at all. Their faces are not looking your way! When God says **He "always faces us"** He is communicating the reality of a personal relationship.

Recently there have been changes in our ministry through personnel, changing of school schedules, limitation of time constraints of individuals to participate in ministry activity, and personally facing the lack of control…which is terrible when you are a control freak! I am not really discouraged with my family, ministry, or surroundings. I seem to be more discouraged with myself.

> *"When you are in the dark, listen and God will give you a message to share with others when you get in the light."* —Oswald Chambers

Once a physician let Judy and me stay at their place in Florida. At night when depression seems so dark, I found myself standing as close to the sea as the incoming waves would allow. I could not help noticing a full moon as I listened to the thunder of the surf. I noticed a series of huge breakers when the moonlight would dance across the foam, tumbling upon itself and swishing far up to the sand. And then…the sea would calm and the streak of light from the moon would lie flat with a brilliant sheen all the way across the wet sand…to my feet. That is amazing! The sea and the moon are putting on a private show for me. Just for me! If I step this way the streak stays with me. If I jump the other way, it is there too. If I run down the beach, the streak of light kept right before me…it never stopped. It was never too late.

Then I thought to myself, "Well, Earle, this is what God…is to you, isn't it?" God was saying, "Earle, *my face* is your way. You can run as fast as you can, you can travel as far as you like, you can hide as long as you will, but *my face* will always be toward you. I will never turn away."

Omnipresent! "It makes no difference what your circumstances are, twisted and troubled like the riptide or completely calm and at rest. *My face* is still your way. All that I am is yours…to dispel the darkness." I found myself praying…if this is so, the moon shows me more glory when the sea is most troubled. Could it be that you are best seen in those times too?

> **"But we all, with unveiled face, beholding as in a mirror the Glory of the Lord, are being transformed into the same image from Glory to Glory just as from the Lord, the Spirit."** 2 Corinthians 3:18

Perhaps this very moment you are grappling with loneliness, discouragement, and hopelessness. Hope seems so distant, so unreachable, but remember…**God is facing you!** Right now, picture the moonlight on the sea and know all that God is…is…**in your face!**

---•••---

SOVEREIGNTY, SECURITY...CERTAINTY?

"Security" and "uncertainty"...they don't seem to go together. We feel sovereignty should give us a firm sense of certainty and not perplexity.

But in the mind of God, it is apparently not so...

It is true that sovereignty brings security. Knowing that God is in *control* of everything (Romans 8:28) and He has *purposed* everything (Isaiah 46:8-11) gives you a tremendous security. But some seek more than security...out of the doctrine of sovereignty.

They want specific directions, clear guidance...they want certainty!

We want to know what God has purposed in detail for our professions, family, personal goals. We want God's sovereignty to take all the uncertainty out of life. But it doesn't...why?

Because we are to live by faith. **Faith is ridiculous!** Because it is far easier to walk by sight than insight, especially Divine insight.

Consider Jericho...anyone skilled in the art of military warfare would have known they were to: 1. Scale the walls; 2. Batter in the gates; 3. Lay a siege to the city.

Simple...but God's ways are not man's ways because He gave a fourth. That is where **faith seems ridiculous.** What did God do? He told Joshua, "March around the city once a day for six days. Blow the ram's horn and carry a little wooden box. Then, on the seventh day, do it seven times!"

Seems ridiculous, doesn't it?

No one else had ever taken a city that way... because they couldn't find this military strategy in anyone's history. It looked ridiculous.

They acted on God's word, then what happened...nothing! That's the most embarrassing part. Imagine if you were there for six days and nothing happened. But God said it would work not on the third, fifth, or sixth day but on the seventh. The Israelites had to feel ridiculous to the world for six days.

"God is independent of all, but all are dependent upon Him. He can do without us...we can't do without

Him!"

Faith is not ridiculous to those who exercise it, but often our faith appears to be very ridiculous to others—until it works. And they are found without it. If you are going to live by faith, as we have been trusting Jesus for our finances, join us in being certain in our uncertainties!

A sovereign God is unknowable unless He chooses to reveal Himself. He has done this with Jesus: "If you have seen Me, you have seen the Father." Jesus is the final revelation.

Rest in His security, and be reckless in your uncertainty!

—•••—

CLAY POTS

Are you…a pot?

    or

           a passageway?

              …a thoroughfare

                or

                  a dead-end?

…a channel through which your life overflows to that of another? A means…not just an end-all?

> **"Woe to the one who quarrels with his Maker—an earthenware vessel among the vessels of earth! Will the clay say to the potter 'What are you doing?' Or the thing you are making say, 'He has no hands?' "**
> Isaiah 45:9

God's messenger Isaiah says, "A vessel of clay may be the instrument of Deity. Don't gripe if you are clay and not gold"; a servant not just a doctor. Not a reservoir but an outlet; not a storehouse but a pumping station.

We pray "Lord, use me." We need to pray "Lord, make me useable. . . and lovable."

"Love is the overflow of joy in God…that meets the needs of others." —John Piper

Jacob (the trickster) had to be broken clay…before he became named Israel of God.

Peter had to be humbled by utter failure…before being used to love Jesus and His sheep.

Saul was brought to the ground crying to Jesus, "Lord what would you have me to do…to be?"

Think about it.

What does God use? Small things in His hands are greatly used.

Moses	Gideon	David	Peter	Small Boy
|	|	|	|	|
his Rod	300 men with clay pots and lamps	1 sling shot, 5 stones	his boat	5 loaves, 2 fish

"But we have this treasure in earthen vessels, that the surpassing **greatness of the power may be of God and not from ourselves.**" 2 Corinthians 4:7

Are you willing to "**be a clay pot**" through which Jesus' power will flow? A serviceable tool in the hand of the wise potter doesn't question "Stop! Why are you using me this way?" Little is much with God in it!

— ••• —

WISDOM

Proverbs is an amazing book in the Bible. It bares out general truths about life. There is no halo…no official saints…no theoretical Christianity in Proverbs. The problems of reality in shoe leather Christianity stand out.

The first nine chapters are set in the context of the father giving counsel to his son. How can you impress your son with the importance of wisdom? The father describes wisdom as a very desirable woman—not sexually desirable but desirable for her fine life and the good she offers. We may call her Lady Wisdom. He also describes the woman of this world as an alluring, sexy woman who, like a prostitute, seeks to lure young men into her trap.

He wants his son to be married to Lady Wisdom and not to Mistress Evil!

Solomon remembers in Proverbs 7 what happened to his father, David. He knows the tendency of his own feeble heart…watches the addiction of his own sons…does all he can to shout out warnings concerning the dangers of playing with the fire of adultery.

"My son, keep...treasure...bind...write my words that they may keep you from the strange woman." (v. 1-5)

The young man is immature...untaught...and unprotected, becoming a sitting duck, an easy prey. He did not have plans for the evening hours..."in the abundance of idleness."

Idle nights are always an inlet to fleshly temptations.

Look at the woman doing the tempting. She is married but unfaithful—sensually dressed...crafty in her approach...talkative and self-willed...externally religious, internally rotten. "Her house is the way to Sheol" (27)!

Verses 22-23 tell of this man being shot "with a piercing arrow" as an ox...as a fool... as a bird! As an ox, he thinks he is going to feast in green pastures, and he is being led to the slaughterhouse. As a fool, he thinks he is going to play and have a great time, and he is being chained. As a bird, he thinks he is going to eat some easy food, and he is being caught in the teeth of the trap.

So many in the medical/dental profession have fallen in this battle. With decayed character, destroyed morals, and diseased souls, they have become like department store merchandise "slightly soiled, greatly reduced in value."

The best defense against the lust of the flesh? The Word of God. Wisdom is not simply wise sayings. It is applying what God has said in His Word to every facet of your life.

The wisdom of the world is the collective opinions of men about what is best for them. What seems foolish to the world is the very means God has established to save men. Prove to be wise in God's sight while fools to the world...believe in Jesus.

"For the word of the cross is to those who are perishing foolishness, but to us who are being saved, it is the power of God." 1 Corinthians 1:18

What the world despises...wisdom from God...we must desire.

———•••———

THE CROSS—FOOLISHNESS OF GOD

"For the story of the Cross is shear absurdity to those who are per-
ishing, but to those that are being saved, it's the manifestation of the
power of God. The world and its earthly wisdom failed to perceive
God by means of its own philosophy. God in His wisdom was pleased
through the foolishness of the Cross to save...those who believe."
1 Corinthians 1:18,21

The Scripture says of King Hezekiah (2 Kings 18–20) that he "did what was right in the sight of the Lord," according to all that his father, David, had done since he had removed the high places and the pillars, cut down the Asherah, and most importantly broke in pieces the bronze serpent that Moses had made. Israel had worshipped the bronze serpent as an idol.

Some 700 years before in Numbers 21:8-9, the Lord told Moses to make a fiery serpent, then set it on a standard. Everyone who looked at it and was bitten would live. Moses made that serpent, and that's exactly what happened. They like us having been bitten with the sin of rebellion; they

—Believed God's Word,

—Looked on the serpent and then lived!

This is the "type" of what was to come with Christ's death on the Cross.

"The Cross is not the Cross of a martyr: It is a mirror of the nature of God...focused in one
point of history." —Oswald Chambers

This is confirmed in John 3:14,15, when it quotes how Moses lifted up the serpent. So, the Son of Man must be lifted up so that whoever believes may have eternal life.

"The Cross of Christ means the salvation of God goes deeper down than the deepest depths of in-
iquity...man can commit. No man can get beyond the reach of Jesus." —Oswald Chambers

Each of us has been bitten, even in the womb, by the serpent of sin. Isn't it amazing that God has taken the foolish things of this world, the death of His Son on the Cross to shed blood for our sins, to take the punishment we deserve, to die in our place...in order to give us eternal life?

What are the high places in your life that you are trying to medicate with the bite of sin? There is only one solution to this. Your willful choice *"to look"* (as the Israelites did to the serpent that was lifted up) at Christ.

Foolishness? Yes, it is. Isn't it amazing how one decision we make now *"to look"* to the Cross, makes a difference in our eternal destiny!

In the days of universalism, Acts shouts out so clearly, "There is no other name under heaven by which man can be saved…but Jesus."

Look to the Cross!

———•••———

COMFORT

"I, even I, am He who comforts you. Who are you that you are afraid of man? He dies!" Isaiah 51:12

God protects… where we are exposed.

Do we want comfort or comfortable living? Society has produced great comforts of home, air-conditioning, luxurious food, and many other extras that help make living a little more enjoyable, but they don't necessarily give internal comfort.

God's comfort is a far cry from luxurious things or mental power of positive thinking. God does not remove the cross in our lives, but He gives us strength to bear it. He doesn't take away the battle, but He gives us peace in the midst of war. He doesn't remove adversities, but He gives us courage to endure.

We are swept off our feet by the death of a loved one, and we are plunged into despair by poor health; financial reverses shatter hopes, and when all seems lost, we need to sense a new and invigorated resource. Why not count on **"I, even I, am He who comforts you"**?

A noted physician left a note penned to his pillow before committing suicide:

"I've had few difficulties, many friends, great successes; I've gone from wife to wife, from home to home, visited many countries of the world, but I'm fed up with invented devices to fill up 24 hours of each day."

Comfortless! Influential in medicine yet lonely, burdened, and a discouraged person. Comfort to him had become associated with using luxury, whereas the original meaning of "comfort" suggests "impregnable protection of a mountain fortress."

> *"Blessed be the God and Father of our Lord Jesus Christ, the Father of mercies, and the God of all comfort; who comforts us in all our affliction so that we may be able to comfort those who are in any affliction with the comfort with which we ourselves are comforted by God."*
> 2 Corinthians 1:3-4

Comfort of prayer…came when I was asked (four days beforehand) to fill in for the Governor of Alabama at the Dental State Convention Prayer Luncheon in Montgomery. Prayers enabled me to present the Gospel in a way that was applicable to the felt needs of the dentists. The comment cards revealed the power of prayers—for two people trusted Christ, several said they were glad that the scheduled speaker couldn't come, and one lady said, "That was just what I needed to hear."

"When God comforts His people, He makes them strong in weakness."

Our ministry is to create an environment of comfort that is an extension of the comfort God has provided to us.

—•••—

A SIGH

Jesus is a study of contrast. In Mark 7:24-30, Jesus heard the problem of the Gentile's Syrophoenician mother's request to cast the demon out of her daughter. She pleaded. He heard. He did not touch. He spoke the word. The daughter was healed.

Then in Mark 7:31-37, there was a request of a man who couldn't hear. Jesus heard the request. This time he touched his lips. The man was healed. Look at the passage:

> *"At the Sea of Galilee there were some people who brought to Jesus a man who was deaf and spoke with difficulty, and they begged Him to place His hand upon him. After He took him aside, away from the crowd, Jesus put His fingers into the man's ears. Then He spit and touched the man's tongue. He looked up into heaven and with a deep*

sigh said to him "Ephphatha!" (which means "Be opened!"). At this the man's ears were opened, his tongue was loosened, and he began to speak plainly."

Quite a passage, isn't it?

Jesus is presented with a man who is deaf and has a speech impediment. Perhaps he stammered. Maybe he spoke with a lisp. Perhaps, because of his deafness, he never learned to articulate words properly.

Jesus refused to exploit the situation, so He took the man aside. He looked him in the face. Knowing it would be useless to talk, He explained what He was about to do through gestures. He spat and touched the man's tongue, telling him that whatever restricted his speech was about to be removed. He touched his ears. They, for the time, were about to hear.

But before the man said a word or heard a sound, Jesus did something I never would have anticipated.

He sighed! Whatever you might have expected—a song or a prayer or a praise—the Son of God did none of these. Instead, He paused…looked into Heaven…and sighed. From the depths of his being came a rush of emotion that said more than words.

Sigh. The word seems out of place. Have you ever thought of God as one who sighs?

I counseled a young couple in which the husband wanted to resolve the marriage problem and the wife did not. As his wife listened to me explain how these things could be reconciled, there was no comment. They left; I did not know if they would be back. I sighed.

The bright-eyed, dirty-faced, scantily-dressed four-year-old girl in the North Philadelphia area where S.M.I. students were giving immunizations one summer asked me to hold her. I held her. She would not let me put her down for two hours. I eventually had to put her down as I left. She ran after our van, waving. As I looked back, I sighed.

I sighed today listening to a wife tell how her husband will not cut back on his schedule to be with her.

If you have had teenagers, you probably have sighed from your motives being questioned or your best acts of love being rejected. The "sigh" of Jesus is a sigh of frustration and sadness that lies somewhere between a fit of anger and a burst of tears.

All these sighs come from a recognition of pain that was never intended or of hope deferred.

When Jesus looked into the eyes of Satan's victim the only perfect thing to do was to sigh. It was never intended to be this way, the sigh said. Your ears were not made to be deaf. Your tongue was not made to stumble. God's sigh is His indirect way of saying that God's pain is our comfort. He has felt the burden for what was not intended.

The "Holy sigh" assures us that God still groans for His people. **He groans for the day when all sighs will cease and when what was intended to be…will be.**

—•••—

THE FRIENDSHIP OF GRACE

Is Grace a blue-eyed blonde? No, Grace is like a diamond with multiple facets. It is not simply a one-time acquaintance…it is daily quenching of your thirst. Grace is a loyal friend at these times in my life.

First, when I am hurting.

We do not know what Paul's "thorn in the flesh" actually was, but it pierced him deeply, constantly reminding him of his inadequacy. It spawned fears, raised doubts, perhaps even caused physical pain. When Paul said he felt the most worthless did the Father condemn him because of his weakness? NO! Grace accepts and understands.

> *"My grace is sufficient for you…*
> *for my power is perfected in weakness."* 2 Corinthians 12:9

Grace provides comfort not criticism; it reaches out to support us not tear us down. Grace is our enthusiastic friend, the one who makes us sufficient…in our weakness and pain.

Second, when I am weak and unable to stand firm.

Temptation stalks each of us. It never quits, never tires of assaulting its victims until it finds a weakness, wears us down, and then comes in for the kill. Have you felt like you are giving ground in a losing battle? We feel discouraged. We are weak, tired, and ready to quit. What are we supposed to do? Quit this group and join another? Go for disability? No.

> *"Draw near with confidence to the throne of grace to find mercy and*

grace to help...in our time of need. "Hebrews 4:15-16

Draw near...don't be afraid...enjoy your need.

Third, Grace preserves me in a perverse generation.

Steadfastness is that straight and narrow path we walk in the midst of a crooked and perverse generation. But how? To keep from tripping, look at Peter's prescription to maintain a balance in Grace and Knowledge...of our Lord. But watch it! It may be easy to grow in Knowledge and not in Grace (2 Peter 3:17-18).

Knowledge without Grace can be a terrible weapon. And Grace without knowledge can be very shallow. But put them together and we have a moral tool for building our lives.

Growing in Grace means becoming more like Jesus. Challenging. Peter, who denied the Lord and who was weak, helpless, and fearful, knew Grace in ways he never would have without those emotions. He will take your pain, your troubles, your fears, your angers, your shortcomings, to the God of all Grace.

The God of all Grace who called you to His eternal Glory in Christ will Himself perfect, confirm, strengthen, and establish you. 1 Peter 5:10

To live the Christian life means failure, joy, forgiveness, misunderstandings, sin as well as victories and accomplishment. Grace is the friend for which I am grateful.

I commend this friendship to you...Grace.

—•••—

REFUELING

"In sitting down He called the twelve and said to them, 'If anyone wants to be first...he shall be last...of all and servant of all.' "
Mark 9:35

In God's sight many bulky things are very little...and many small things are very great. The reason is that God sees the heart and the hidden springs of action there, and He judges the streams by the fountain. Quantity is nothing to Him unless there be zeal, and zeal is nothing to Him unless it be purged from all self-seeking and vain glory. God wants a pure spring of impulses and a pure flame of devotion. He wants us to have a sacrificial love for others as Jesus had.

Sacrificial love has one problem: If you commit yourself to it you will find that it is extremely exhausting. After a certain amount of giving, serving, expending, you begin to feel numb as though you have nothing left to give. You are running on empty. However, it is possible to love people not only sacrificially but also steadfastly. He wants us to learn how to refuel ourselves in the spiritual, emotional, and physical aspects of our lives.

David displays the **spiritual refueling** in 1 Samuel 30, where it says, "David encouraged himself in the Lord his God for his tank was almost dry when enemy forces had ambushed his camp carrying off the wives and children of David and his men." In this situation, he wanted to pitch his leadership position and would have lied to check out. What could he do?

He took time out, got away by himself, and had a l-o-n-g talk with God. He spent time in solitude with God until the spiritual energy supply was replenished. We need to make opportunities in our schedules to sit down, get off the treadmill, and seek out solitude to encourage ourselves in God. We need to have a daily time of solitude before the events of the day rush in. Talk...read...allow God to regenerate your spiritual energies.

The next is **emotional refueling.** You can replenish your emotional tank so you won't maintain that uninterested feeling in the well-being of others by "relaxation and recreation." Many prefer to get relaxation from a pill or an injection; however, why not find a place to stop for 15 minutes on the way home to take a break, take deep breaths, and restore your emotional strength? You might find a corner of your home where you would be alone. A couple of hours of recreational activities can refuel you emotionally to make it possible for you to go back to loving others steadfastly and sacrificially.

The last thing is **physical refueling.** If you get your spiritual and emotional tanks full and you still feel like hiding under your desk when you hear the incessant footsteps of more patients, you may need to check your physical fuel gauge. It takes physical energy to listen, to serve, to confront, to rebuke. A sign of weakness in this area is if you are easily irritated, critical, short-fused, sensitive, and negative. To solve this, follow three rules: Eat right, sleep enough, and exercise.

Where is the leisureliness that doesn't smack of laziness? Solitude that produces soul growth? Seek silence in your life. Silence not only is beneficial to sanity and intellectual labor but also helps man live a life that reaches from the depths...to the heights.

"Let avoidable noise be avoided."

It is in silence that God's mysterious voice is best heard.

———•••———

THE WHEELS OF PROVIDENCE

Why do things happen that bring so much sorrow and heartache?

Is it true that our disappointments are often God's appointments?

> ***"To everything there is a Season, and a 'Time' to Every purpose. . . under Heaven."*** Ecclesiastes 3:1

Be assured. . . there are no mere accidents in your life.
> In this world of perpetual change
>> …fluctuating events
>>> …and shifting circumstances.

Isn't it great to have a stable center that says:

> ***"My 'Times' are in…His Hands."*** Psalm 31:15

Our loving Father has obligated Himself that everything that takes place in the lives of those who love Him is for our good. Are you sure? Is Romans 8:28 true? It says:

> ***"And we know that for those who love God all things work together for good."***

Ecclesiastes 3:2-8 gives situations that cover the rampart of events that come into our lives. Read the List!

•Industrial Relations	•Life and Death
•Human Labor	•Fun and Sorrow
•Public Service	•War and Peace
•Social/Business	•Feelings

All these must be seen in the light of…

> *"All the wheels of Providence rolling along on the highway of Divine purposes"*
> —Charles Spurgeon

What are the lessons for our hearts from Solomon's experiences?

First of all, there is no fatalism here. Your confidence must be based upon a practical dependence on God. The God who created you, chose you, is intensely interested in you, loves you first and unconditionally…loves passionately!

Secondly, face the reality of our impotency and inconsistency. The human clay is frail and weak. It breaks…comes unglued very easily.

Finally, look at the Creator NOT the creature.

He makes no mistakes. Nothing happens behind His back nor with His eyes closed. In all of life there is the perfection of His harmony and purposes.

"All sunshine and blue skies make for a Sahara Desert."

Jesus Christ is the Completer…
    of unfinished people…
        with unfinished work…
            in unfinished times.

Are you recognizing the wheels of His providence?

---•••---

WHO IS ABLE?

Now to Him…who is able to do exceedingly abundantly beyond all that we ask or think. . . according to the power that works within us.
Ephesians 3:20

The point of this mind-boggling prayer is to be found in the preposition "Kata," which means "according to." God ministers to us His grace and blessings "according to" the power that works within us.

When "Kata" is in the Greek accusative case, it "illustrates an object bending toward another in order to meet its need." God's power bends toward us to work in us…to fill us to be full with His blessing. The human side of the individual prayer life (to ask) is met by the divine side—God's power working within us.

"We ask much and think little…but He does more and thinks greater."

The privilege of prayer is found in the "ask or petition." The extent of prayer is suggested by the word "think." The supply of prayer is discovered in the "abundantly." The overflow of prayer is revealed in the "exceedingly abundantly" of the super-abundance that goes beyond—the super-abundance of God's giving!

The encouragement of prayer is revealed in the "God is able" in one of the descriptive names of God...El Shaddai, which depicts His sufficiency. The word Shad means breast—portraying the unfailing supply of nurture—the basic necessity of life. Rest... lie on His chest!

Prayer is either a prodigious force or disgraceful farce. If a farce, you may pray much and get little; if a force, you may pray little and get much. —Dr. A.F. Schauffler

Nehemiah, a man of prayer, received the report of the broken-down walls and gates in Jerusalem. God's principle is "you never will lighten the load unless first you have felt the pressure in your own soul." God must open your eyes to see things as they are. Nehemiah started weeping...and then began working. After Nehemiah's despair there came determination. Nehemiah mourned over the ruins, which invoked dependence on God.

I am feeling the broken walls in our society and spiritual warfare affecting us and our children. There is absolutely no winning without warfare...no opportunity without opposition...no victory without vigilance.

Who is able?

He is able...to do exceedingly abundantly, beyond all that we ask or think, according to...He who is able!

CHAPTER FOUR

WORSHIP

———•••———

RADICAL LOVE

What does it mean to love with **Christ's radical love?**

"Teach me, Father, how to love the most
Those who stand in need of love—the host
Of people who are sick and poor and bad
Whose tired faces show their lives are sad." —Beatrice Cleland

Isn't an unkind Christian a contradiction? Kindness is a fabric of a secure person. . . the sympathetic nature is not weak or woeful but a sincere attitude of love toward others. Kindness is love in the active voice; long suffering is love in the passive.

Jesus in the Sermon on the Mount speaks not to "actions" alone, but he focuses on "attitudes" as shown by stating, "You have heard it said, but I say to you." Read Matthew 5:38-42 and notice three things: One, if someone strikes you on your right cheek, turn him the other; two, if anyone wants to sue you and take your shirt, let him have your coat; three, whoever would force you to go one mile, go with him two.

A slap in the face demands a radical response, for there is ultimate degradation of your honor at stake. The implication is that your honor may not be the most important thing in the world. With legal rights you are to be non-retaliatory, for revenge escalates animosity, and when you are pressed into extra service, Jesus expects that we would exceed the bare minimum.

If you show compassion only to those who are worthy of it, that is no great sacrifice. Supposing God showed kindness only to those who deserved it...where would we be? As tough as it is, we are to love our enemies, and we are to do deeds of kindness to the stubborn, the rebellious, the hostile. Kindness is never artificial. Its genuineness is proven by the willing sacrifice

...for the kindness that costs nothing is usually worth nothing.

You will find yourself out in deep water with Christ when you...

Take slaps
Give up your legal rights
And you carry burdens a lot farther than
you need to carry them.

Most people never leave the harbors of love to venture out on the high seas of radical, non-retaliatory, second-mile love. That's where radical love is experienced!

God's presence manifests itself in "deep waters" not as a "shore-bound" Christian. If we will live this way, people will be startled into taking a closer look at Jesus Christ, hostilities die, and lasting peace will ensue.

Look today for an opportunity to relieve the sick, comfort someone in sorrow. Help bear the load of another person who is staggering, or by kindness and quietness of your speech, quiet an upset friend. Kindness is not the effeminate expression of weakness but the demonstration of gentleness of strength.

Can you do this? Will you? Radical love does not make sense. **Radical love is not easy. . . it is supernatural.**

— ••• —

A FATHER

If you could paint an accurate picture of the god you worship, would I like him? Each of us has a "God-image"—a picture of God in our minds. For some of us the image is good, for others…distorted.

 Behind every theological problem and most psychological problems lies a wrong view of God.

"Worshipers become like the god they worship."

Our view of God as our Father is dependent upon our view of our human father. **Do you see God as He actually is…or as you think He is?**

Jesus encountered a "God-image" problem with the Pharisees. In Luke 15:1-2, Jesus associated intimately with publicans and prostitutes. They came very near Him "to listen." The Pharisees "grumbled," for their view of God would not have contact with sinners.

Jesus challenged the Pharisees' "God-image" by painting a picture of God in order to puncture their wrong perception.

The first parable pictures God as a **Determined Shepherd** who cares for the lost individual. Jesus died for individuals, not for a group.

In verses 8-10, we see a **Diligent Woman** who lost one of the ten coins from her dowry. We see God as a searching woman who values the significance of a lost item. The value of something is dependent upon what someone is willing to pay for it. What is your value? 1 Peter says it is the "precious blood of God's only Son"… an infinite sacrifice for something of infinite value.

The last parable (v. 11-32) shows God as a **Devoted Father.** Note the father is willing to allow his son to travel to the far country with his inheritance. A principle:

**"God gives you the freedom to choose even when
He knows that which we choose is not best."**

The son comes to his senses. As with him, the most sensible thing for us to do is to admit we sinned and come back home. The father, who looked every day for his son to come back home, ran to meet his son. "The father saw him and felt compassion for him and ran and embraced him and kissed him." The father interrupts the confession of the son to show his acceptance by giving him a robe (honor), a ring (authority), and sandals (he was a son and not a slave).

The older son, who is an analogy of a Pharisee, stayed home. Although his hands were on the farm, his heart was in the far country. His anger is evident when the father entreats him to come and celebrate.

God does not want us to harbor false images of who He is; He strips those falsehoods from us. It is better to live naked in truth than clothed in fantasy. Healing our image of God heals our image of ourselves. Within so many of us is a little girl or boy crying out for love and acceptance…because we have experienced rejection or abandonment from our father.

Jesus frees us from the fear of the Father and dislike of ourselves.

How do you heal this false image of God? There are two tools God has given us to transform our "God-image."

   • **The Word of God** (2 Timothy 3:16-17). You learn what God is like by reading about Him in the Scriptures.

   • **The Body of Christ** (John 13:34-35). As you see the character of God "fleshed out" by members of the Body of Christ, you learn what God is really like.

How do you really picture God? Do you receive or reject sinners…even yourself? When you hate yourself, are you willing to let Him embrace you with His love? Why not crawl up in His lap and enjoy His love?

"You cannot think wrongly and live rightly;
you cannot believe error and practice truth."

•••

GOD CAN'T STOP THINKING OF YOU

In the midst of life's stress, we need to be reminded of the mind of God toward us. He assures us that we are never out of His thoughts…and always close to His heart. Never out of His thoughts!

There is never a time when He is indifferent to our pain or unresponsive to our needs.

> *"How precious also are Thy thoughts to me, O God! How great is the sum of them! If I should count them…they are more in number than the sand. When…I awake. I am still with Thee."* Psalm 139:17-18

His arms are always open.
His ears are always listening.
His eyes are always watching.
His heart is always loving.

There is never a time when you are not in His thoughts,
Never a time without His grace,
Never a time when He turns away from any need you face.

> *"Can a mother forget the baby at her breast and have no compassion on the child she has borne? Though she may forget, I will not forget you!"* Isaiah 45:15

> *"You know when I sit down and when I rise up; you discern my thoughts from afar. You search out my path and my lying down and are acquainted with all my ways. Even before a word is on my tongue, behold, O Lord, you know it altogether. You hem me in, behind and before, and lay your hand upon me. Such knowledge is too wonderful for me; it is high; I cannot attain it."* Psalm 139:2-6

God is working in more ways than you have asked Him. He is doing more things for you than your faith can imagine!

> *" 'For I know the plans that I have for you,' declares the Lord, 'plans for welfare and not for calamity to give you a future and a hope.' "*
> Jeremiah 29:11

You are not here by chance. You are here at this time to fulfill His purpose…for these patients…for your family.

God is always ahead of you.

He loved you—even before you gave your heart to Him.

He provided all things—even before you had a need.

He knew all things—even before you had a question.

He gave Himself—even before He asked you to touch others.

> *"He will not allow your foot to slip; He who keeps you will not slumber. Behold, He who keeps Israel will never slumber nor sleep."*
> Psalm 121:3-4

The troubled surface of a lake will not reflect an object clearly. Likewise, the image of God is seen the clearest when we are at rest… in Him, when we put our souls before Him. Stop. Think of Him. Rest. He is always thinking of you.

"If God stopped thinking of you, He would cease to exist."

•••

THE LOVE OF MONEY

Can't live without it…but how can you live with it? Individuals ruin their health, shipwreck their homes, sacrifice their lives, and forfeit their integrity for money.

> *"God has given to some people very great wealth and honor so they can have everything they want 'but though a man lives a thousand years twice over but doesn't find contentment' well, what is the use."*
> Ecclesiastes 6:2,6

Some people worship money...some make it an idol. Some beg, some borrow, some steal it. A few inherit money; others marry it. The majority of us work for it. We all spend it. We all want more of it. Do you agree?

The love of money is the root of all kinds of evil.

If you agree, you are agreeing with Scripture. Jesus, who was so gentle and compassionate, was hard-hitting on the proposition of "you cannot serve God and mammon." What is the problem? Money promises what it can never produce. Get wealth and you will have prosperity and peace, one thinks. That is just not true!

What can money do for you? Its roads are full of mirages—enticing gleams of water that vanish as soon as we draw near. Depressingly, the alluring pools turn out to be hot, glowing sand piles, which lead you only to intensify your thirst.

God gives to some the honor of having riches, but He would give to all His loved ones the wealth of a "contented" life. This is wealth without a limit. The subject of 1 Timothy 6 says everybody lives in two tents: "content or discontent." Look deeper in verse 17:

> ***"Command those who are rich in this present world (1) not to be arrogant and (2) not to put their hope in wealth, which is so uncertain, but (3) to put their hope in God, who richly provides us with everything for our enjoyment."***

Enjoy?

Amazing! God, who has richly supplied you, expects you to even enjoy it! He doesn't stop there but he says for those who are rich...to be rich in good works, to be generous and ready to share, storing up for themselves the treasure of a good foundation for the future so they may take hold of that which is life indeed. Be known by the things you love!

"Anything can be a tool or an idol."

What you bend your knee to is what you worship. The issue is not what you have, not what you own, but what owns you. You can't take it with you, but you can send it ahead...giving out of the Grace you have been given. Do the right thing for the right reason!

The dial on the thermometer tells you how hot something is; money can be God's thermometer. How hot are you?

———•••———

IDOLS

"He who loves money will not be satisfied with money, nor he who loves abundance with his income. This too is vanity. When good things increase, those who consume them increase. So what is the advantage of the owners except to look on? Or except to see with their eyes?"
Ecclesiastes 5:10-11

Idolatry is not limited to the pagans of the darkest jungles or the worshippers of a Buddha-God. The start of idolatry is…whenever a person longs for what they dare not do…hungers after what they must not have…lusts for what they have no business loving.

Man must worship…It's our nature. It's built in. If you aren't worshiping the one and only true God, then the heart will invent its own god…or gods! Any object that produces passionate devotion is an imposter. God allows for no rivals. The Israelites cast a calf then grew very festive over what their own hands had manufactured. To make something and then bow down before it is **Idolatry.** To love success, ambition, prominence, and position is to retain an idol upon the throne of your heart. It is not the having it but the loving it that is wrong.

When gadgets become our gods…watch out! Man cannot live by bread alone nor procedures or lasers or crowns or surgical cures. Three tempting and fascinating idols are: **Gold, Good Times, and Goods.**

Gold…you can pursue it, yet it will not maintain satisfaction. Do not remove the **Idol** and not turn in love to God…this will leave a bad taste in your soul called dissatisfaction. The "thing" is gone, but the appetite is still there. Or even worse…an empty void.

Good times…eat, drink, and be merry; worship at the throne of levity and enjoyment. Paul warns youthful Timothy that men in the future would be *"lovers of pleasure more than lovers of God"* (2 Timothy 3:4).

Goods…anything can be a tool or an idol; what we hold on to we treasure in life. Do you possess them, or them you? Who is in control?

Excessive love for anything proves God's first commandment: "Thou shalt not have any other gods before Me." Man must worship…it's our nature; what price are you paying for **gold, goods, or a good time?**

You can love…**Gold** yet it will not satisfy, love **Goods** with abundance of things, and **Good times** by positions and professional popularity. What good are they but to behold and use?

Love Jesus, and leave them. You can't serve two masters.

———•••———

THOROUGHLY CLEAN

"His winnowing fork is in His hand, and He will thoroughly clear His threshing floor…" Matthew 3:12

Nehemiah was a picture of "thoroughness" in everything he undertook. He was all aglow and always on the go. Difficulties did not daunt him, nor opposition haunt him. He was not half-hearted, nor would he allow any compromise for one moment.

The believer does not need to have the hesitancy of half-heartedness or the vacillation of compromise or being unequally yoked with unbelievers or even the nauseousness of lukewarmness.

"Christ always cleans out before He comes in. He fits before He furnishes. He empties before He fills. He cleanses before He conforms. He purifies before he possesses."

A wild man, who lived in the woods, became a friend to a wildcat. Finding the cat in a trap, he released it, but its leg was broken. The cat would not leave the wild man but followed him, "trailing a limb."

There are many Christian people like the cat. Saved? Of course, they are saved, but they "trail a limb." That is the one thing you notice about them. You forget the brightness of the eyes; everything is taken up with the "trailing limb."

How many people are not enjoying the Christian life because of the pathology of their past, the pain of which they attribute their bad temper in the present? How can they "love the Lord" and yet be in disobedience to known revelation?

Do you have a "trailing limb"? God's gracious ministry can remove the cataract from your **eye** of faith…so you can see clearly. He can cleanse the **ear** from stoppage…

so you can hear and obey. He can take out the sting from an unholy **tongue**...so gracious words like Jesus' will drop from your lips to heal. He can purify our **hearts** from every contaminating thing so we will be a place for His Shekinah glory.

> *"Shining is always costly. Light comes only at the cost of that which produces it. An unlit candle does no shining. Burning must come before shining. We cannot be of great use to others without cost to ourselves. Burning suggests suffering. We shrink from pain...'the glory of tomorrow is rooted in the drudgery of today.'"*
> Streams in the Desert —Mrs. Charles Cowman, p.128

Many want the glory without the cross, the shining without the burning; the crucifixion comes before coronation.

What is the motivation? See clearly the love of God. It is not that I know God, but the fact that He knows me...because...

> I am engraved on the palms of His hands...
> I am never out of His mind...
> I know Him because He first knew me.

> *"There is tremendous relief in knowing that His love to me is utterly realistic, based at every point on prior knowledge of the worst about me so that no discovery can disillusion Him about me."*
> —J.I. Packer

Be thoroughly cleansed. Relax in His love.

———•••———

WHISPERS

"God spreads out the northern skies over emptiness and hangs the earth upon nothing. Yet these are but a small part of His ways or the mere fringes of His force the faintest whisper of His voice! Who then can understand the thunder of His magnificent power?" Job 26:7,14

Creation is a product of God's whisper. What would happen if God roared? The emphasis in Scripture is not so much on God's energy but simply on His words.

"Then God said, 'Let there be light,' and there was light." Genesis 1:3

"*Then God said...and it was so.*" Genesis 1:9,11,14-15

"At the word of the Lord...the heavens were made, and"by the breath of His mouth...all their host." Psalm 33:6

By the mere exercise of His will, God produces whatever He wills. That's omnipotence. God, our Father, is The Great Communicator. His words are His will. His will is His word. His word is power.

When the storm clouds of circumstances gather, what is your reaction? Few of us will admit to the empty feeling in the pit of our stomach; others can label it coming apart at the emotional seams. A small minority may concede life to be a hopeless situation...but for God! My friend Job lived on "Desperation Corner," not knowing which way to turn.

In looking to God for deliverance of any kind we are prone to try to discover what material He has on hand to come to our rescue. When praying for financial help...we are apt to look over the body of Christ to see who we think the Lord will have some influence over to give us money.

It is so human to look and crave for something in sight that will help the Lord out. God's power doesn't need that. In the beginning God created the heavens and the earth out of nothing...absolutely nothing. He hung the earth on nothing! No sky hooks.

"Put communion with God on the throne, and then ask God to direct your common sense to choose according to His will. **Worship first and wits after.*"* —Oswald Chambers

The critical issue is never God's strength...or capacity...or ability. The issue is His **will.** By the mere exercise of His **will,** He produces whatever He wills! Let Him **whisper** to you His promises. How do you get started? Sometimes there will be mysterious ways we simply know that some specific thing is God's will. As we pray we may sense that we are living supernaturally. I doubt if Joshua gave much thought before He asked God to stop the sun. He just knew it was the right thing to do. For most of us these supernatural times don't come very often. God's will for us—the expression of His power in us—is so much bigger than just simply stopping the sun, healing the sickness, or moving the mountains. In fact, it is so gigantic no human being has ever yet comprehended the scope.

"God whispers to us in our joy and shouts to us in our pain. Pain is God's megaphone to get our attention." —C.S. Lewis

The emotional pain that I have experienced in the last two years has communicated who God is and who I am not. Somehow it would not be quite right to have lived our whole lives without ever discovering through times of crisis the greatness of our loving

God…who needs but to "speak the word" and relief is ours!

He will do exactly as He says…in His time…in His way…in His will. Open the Word. Read His Word. Hear His power.

And if you will get still…He will whisper it to you.

———•••———

IN ME

Struggle for peace. Isn't it hard to face up to the storms of life when the boat is sinking? Jesus spoke. It made a difference.

> *"These things I have spoken to you that in Me, you may have peace. In the world, you will have tribulation. But take courage…I have overcome the world."* John 16:33

Amazing, isn't it? Two words **"In Me."** Jesus Christ. You have peace right at the same time you are in the midst of the most violent of storms, shifting circumstances, pain you have for loved ones who have gone to the far country. A multitude of changes overwhelm, such as…

- Family…in conflict, teenagers reacting and rebelling

- Contracts you had with the hospital are not renewed.

- Medicare: Cuts and Cuts and Cuts

- Your income is not increasing. You see more people for less.

- You could move to another city but the situation is worse there.

Is this why you came into medicine? Remember those statements you made at your interview. "I just want to help people!"

Is it true our disappointments are God's appointments? In this world of perpetual change, isn't it great to have a stable center for you to "crawl in the lap" of the great **"In Me"**? Don't try to run away. Do what David did…

> *"Cast your burden on the Lord and He will sustain you: He will never allow the righteous to slip, fail or fall."* Psalm 55:22

Isn't it great to know that He wants it? Not only does He carry the burden, but also He carries us!

So quit being surprised that you have tribulation in the world. The explanation to the haunting question "Why?" is that explanations don't heal but they change the complexion of illness. Four answers to the "Why" question are:

It reminds us that we live in a fallen world.

We realize we desperately need radical dependence on God.

"There is no pit so deep God's love is not deeper still." —Corrie ten Boom

I recognize that I must turn my thoughts to what is certain and clear about God rather than what He has chosen to conceal. Job wanted explanation, but he had a Revelation of God. His friends were looking for reasons.

"So long as you can sweeten another's pain...life is not in vain." —Helen Keller

We are to rejoice in what sufferings can produce.

"The sun that melts the ice hardens the clay.

"All sunshine makes a desert."

"Oh what a happy soul am I! Although I cannot see, I am resolved that in this world contented I will be. How many blessings I enjoy that other people don't...so weep...and sigh because I'm blind, I cannot and I won't." —Fanny Crosby, blind, age 8

Experience Shalom—peace.

Crawl in the lap of your Abba, your daddy. Your **"In Me."**

———•••———

FACE TO FACE

"The Lord spoke to you face to face from the midst of the fire."
Deuteronomy 5:4

Life is affected by the things we see day by day. We usually become what we gaze upon.

"Face to face." Moses knew God so intimately that they lived, walked, talked, fellowshipped together. This conscious and continual presence of God in your life is indispensable. We are changed by beholding. ***"We continue to reflect like mirrors the splendor of the Lord and are being transformed into His likeness"*** (2 Corinthians 3:18).

If you live in gloom, you develop a gloomy outlook. If you live in light, your life is light and bright. Christ's presence lies at the foundation of Christian faith. The more you are persuaded that "in Thy presence is fullness of joy and at Thy right hand are pleasures forevermore" (Psalm 16:10), the more victorious will be your daily experience.

The "presence of God" is what makes the difference in people. Success in life is reached only by steady and constant viewing...face to face...with the Lord Jesus Christ.

—•••—

CLOUDS

As a child I used to love the clouds...guessing what figures they made, wanting to rest in them, to see above them. I didn't know it then, but **clouds** are always connected with God.

"The Lord went out before them by day in a pillar of a cloud by day to lead them on the way." Exodus 13:21

We ought to interpret all of the clouds and mysteries of life in light of our knowledge of God. Often, in adverse circumstances, we are told by others "that we are going through the circumstances to learn something." However, in everything that happens, possibly we should be **unlearning** things that would keep us from living and trusting Jesus.

Moses led the Israelites to the Red Sea. No way out and certainly no way back to Egypt! Haven't you been in this situation? Too many patients, not enough money, too much money, family pressures, children in rebellion, difficult companions to work with, much success, little success.

"The Egyptians were marching after them, and the Israelites were exceedingly frightened and cried out to the Lord." Exodus 14:10

"Clouds" can be viewed as sorrows or sufferings without and within, which seem to dispute the power of God. Think of this: If there were no clouds, we would not need faith. By the clouds, God teaches us to walk by faith.

"And the pillar of the cloud went from before them and stood behind them, and it was a cloud and darkness to the Egyptians but it gave light by night to the Israelites." Exodus 14:20

They were encouraged to move down into the Red Sea. In Luke 9:34, as Peter, John, and James witness Jesus talking to Moses and Elijah, it says, "a cloud came and overshadowed them, and they were afraid as they entered the cloud." **Is there anyone except Jesus in your cloud?** If so, it will get darker, not lighter. At a point in time, you will need to get into the place where there is no one except Jesus. How secure! Is He your shepherd...you shall not want?

"Moses said, 'Stand still and see the salvation of the Lord.'"
Exodus 14:13

Why does God bring thunderclouds and disasters when we want green pastures and still waters?

If we could see behind the clouds...
     ...we find the Father's presence.
          ...behind the lightning—an abiding day that has no darkness.
With a comfort that is unspeakable.

Isn't the medical/dental profession a ministry of triumph over trials? Nowhere else is anyone so involved with protecting, providing, and directing of life. Life is seen as life... death is sought to be defeated.

When the cloud lives in front of you, God provides
...**Direction** Exodus 13:21
When the cloud moves to the rear, God provides
...**Protection** Exodus 14:19-20
In the midst of the clouds it is a place of Divine
...**Revelation** Deuteronomy 31:15

Let us enjoy the...Direction...Protection...Revelation...when it is His pleasure to give them to us.

"God has a purpose in our heartaches,
The Savior always knows what is best;
We learn so many precious lessons,
In each sorrow...trial...and test."

God sends us trials not to impair us but to improve us.

"Don't attach yourself to His gifts…but to the Giver.

When he plunges us into the clouds of night…

Let us press on through the agonizing darkness." —François Fénelon

REST…IN THE CLOUDS

— ••• —

CONCENTRATION

Don't you know when someone has been "beholding the Glory of the Lord"? Can't you feel it in your inner spirit they are reflecting the Lord's character?

Don't be hurried out of your relationship of concentrating on Jesus. Troubles nearly always make us look to God…blessings make us look elsewhere.

> *"But we all, with unveiled face beholding as in a mirror the glory of the Lord…are being transformed into the same image from glory to glory, just as from the Lord, the Spirit."* 2 Corinthians 3:18

What are you concentrating on? Many of us Abba's children are concentrating inwardly on our own lives whether we are co-dependent, insecure, or other multiple pathology. Yes, it is helpful to get counseling or personality tests to consider our weaknesses; however, Jesus would not have us spend most of our time looking within but looking up. The Christian life is a gaze/glance life. We fix our gaze on Jesus. We occasionally glance at our lives.

Where is your gaze? You become like what you focus on.

Concentration is much more valuable than consecration…because consecration is apt to end up as a mere religious sentiment. The busy-ness of duties will knock us out of relationship with God more quickly. Fix your attention on Jesus.

…His beauty,

…His majesty,

…His indescribable love.

Be silent before Him in your concentration, and then be as busy as you like in the ordinary affairs of life.

"I am determined to enjoy Jesus and not endure Christianity."

Concentrate. In silence God confirmed in His Word that I am being transformed from Glory to Glory. I've got glory! You do too! If you trust Jesus.

What are you concentrating on?
> *"If you look at others, you will be. . .Distressed*
> *If you look at yourself, you will be. . .Depressed*
> *If you look at Jesus, you will be. . .Blessed"*

———•••———

THE SIMPLE LIFE

"For I am jealous for you with a godly jealousy; for I betrothed you to one husband, that to Christ I might present you as a pure virgin. But I am afraid, least as the serpent deceived Eve by his craftiness, your minds should be led astray from the simplicity and purity of devotion to Christ." 2 Corinthians 11:2-3

Paul's two "I am"s to the Corinthians are true for us today. "**For I am jealous**"... we are to have a single relationship. "**For I am afraid**" we are to have a single mind. Is your life difficult, complex, and confused? Or is your life simple, supernatural, Jesus Christ? If you have a single relationship and a single mind, you will be experiencing the **simplicity** of the Christian life. Quit trying to figure things out; just be simple and enjoy Jesus' love and His freedom. Since you are betrothed to Christ and He loves you so unconditionally, you can find in your experience that love eliminates doubt... love enables duty. The Greek word for simplicity is "haplotes." It is a compound word that means to fold together, straightness and openness. The New Testament use of simplicity came to mean "to be undivided in your heart or person." Personal wholeness, uncomplicated simplicity. The opposite of simplicity is to be double-minded (dipsychos) as described in James 1:8. Could it be the problems you face in life are because you are double-minded versus single-minded?

The activities of our ministry are to facilitate simplicity, involve you in supernatural provisions, and focus in on Jesus Christ.

"God made me simple; man's complex problems are of his own devising." Ecclesiastes 7:29

Simplicity is well stated in this old Shaker hymn:

"It's a gift to be simple, it's a gift to be free, it's a gift to come down, where we ought to be. And when we see ourselves in a way that's right, we will live in a valley...of love and delight!"

Inward simplicity results in an outward lifestyle.

A college sophomore was sitting at a piano in a corner at a fraternity house. His body was slumped, his face was intent. With the index finger of his right hand, he rhythmically tapped the same key over and over and over again. "What are you doing?" asked a friend, annoyed by the monotony of the one note. "Playing the piano," the sophomore replied. "Well," said his friend, scratching his head and raising his right eyebrow, "everyone I've ever seen play the piano runs his hands all across the keyboard. Like, you know, playing all the keys. Man, I thought that was the way you were supposed to play the piano." Without interrupting his tapping, the sophomore shrugged. "They are looking for it," he said. **"I've found it."**

Have you found simplicity...and purity in devotion to Christ?

———•••———

NEED

Ideals and aspirations are always disturbing. At first, they may be sweetly disturbing; later unless there are resources adequate for their fulfillment, they can lead to a painful sense of frustration...even to despair. The biographies of the great servants of God make it abundantly clear there can be unrest for the Saint as well as unrest for the Sinner. **Have you ever felt an undefined sense of spiritual need?**

Mrs. Howard Taylor has written about her early years in China:

"When I went out to China it was with real consecration to God and a real desire to live for Him only, but out there in China I came to see that there was a great lack in my life. I was often out of touch with the Lord Jesus, often weary, hungry and longing for a blessing. From the first day I landed in China, God began to show me my need by humbling me in the dust. He brought me in contact with other lives who were what I wanted to be."

Is there Something Better?

Yes, I am joined to my Lord in a holy union of love; "I am in Christ," and "Christ is in me"! No union on earth is more real than this mystical union with Christ.

Because of Christ's indwelling, I have Christ's own life within a life that had known experience on earth and, though tempted at all points such as we are, had been without sin. Instead of trying to be in control, I have wanted to be out of control. Instead of praying in times of stress, "Lord, keep me calm," I pray, "Lord, entrench me in your calm."

If God is real, then **He is all we need.** Since he is really there, and He says we are His children, then **He is all we need.**

However, we can be so concerned about our needs that we don't see Him as **"all I need."**

For example, consider the Jews that were following Jesus and listening to His teaching. At one point they became hungry, 5,000 of them. Did Jesus meet **their need?**

Yes, but having fed them, He began to teach them:

> *"I am the bread of life...He who eats physical bread will die, but he who eats this Bread shall live forever."* John 6:48-58

What was the response? Many of his disciples WITHDREW...and walked with him no more.

Disciples!

Not His enemies or relatives, but His disciples. They left Him.

Why?

Because they saw that being a disciple was not merely obtaining free lunches or having their **every need** met. Discipleship is an eternal-personal relationship with a living-eternal God.

Discipleship was not a temporal-material, need-oriented relationship with some miracle worker...but a living communion with the Incarnate Son of God. If Jesus is real, then **He is all we need.**

> *"It is the Spirit who gives life; the flesh profits nothing; the words I have spoken to you...are spirit and are life."* John 6:63

The "Life-giving spirit" can free you from your limited reserves to tap the limitless power of the risen Christ.

Is He all you need?

— ••• —

SOLITUDE

The running and the churning person jumps over Proverbs 8:34:

"Blessed is the man who listens to me…watching daily at my gates… waiting at the post of my doors."

For some, this price tag seems too high…listening, watching, and waiting. It is going to take **solitude** so you can hear His voice, watch His movements, and wait for His revealed will. The wise person doesn't have anything to do…but to be! But, I'm post call!

Paradox? Blessed—happy, fortunate to be envied, thrilled with life—is the one who takes time out for inaction. Nothing to do but think!

"Solitude with God repairs the damage done by the fret and noise and clamor of the world."
—Oswald Chambers

Many religious adults are so busy with spreading Christianity that they have little time for quiet meditation and communion with God. Silence and listening to God is substituted with newspapers, books, TV, computers, religious endeavors, and amusements that crowd so much into their lives.

Jesus wants to speak to you. As you open the Word, stop and consider that what you hold is more than paper and ink. You hold the very essence of who Jesus is—his nature, wisdom, guidance, love—distilled into letterform. So, give it permission to roam the rooms of your heart…

Cleaning
Straightening
Rearranging
Closing doors on some things, opening windows on others.

Read with your eyes…but listen with your life.

Has it ever occurred to you that God rested on the seventh day? Was He tired? The God of all power...unfathomable strength! No, rest is a part of the rhythm of His creation. It is to be woven into the fabric of our lives. Cease from your drivenness and turn away from restless pursuits to spend time with Jesus. As your daughter only wants to crawl in your lap and your son to wrestle with you, so God wants time with you. He's waiting. Rest.

'Abba' Father spoke to Jesus once...and the people said it thundered (John 12:29). Jesus didn't agree. His ears were trained by the disposition of His soul to know His Father's voice.

Why not be different? Why not be one who **listens...watches** daily at the gates, and waits at the post of His doors. Will I do what I am recommending to you? Will you? Would it be selfish for me to ask you to pray that I will practice what I preach?

Listen...watch...and wait.

— ••• —

SHALOM (PEACE)

The meaning of "peace" in the Old Testament is wholeness, completeness. Where do you find peace for fractured feelings for fretful doctors?

How is it that Jesus in the midst of opposition from the "Scholars, Scientists, the Learned, the Pharisees, the Sadducees" was able to maintain calm in the midst of the conflict? Jesus, the Prince of Peace, prioritized and found His peace by those early morning times of communication with the Father, His Father. It is a paradox, a physician found out recently who thought she was too busy to find time to be with Jesus...in intimacy with Him when she found the time. Suddenly, the days supernaturally defied her patience amidst the demands so that when all fell down around her in surgery, she was at peace.

How can you have peace...wholeness and completeness...in the midst of the pursuing perplexities of social changes and political correctness? Welcome trials and troubles as friends. Don't resist them as enemies...to your snug way of life.

How can this uncommon philosophy be expressed? Look at Romans 5:3.

"Not only this, but we also exult in our tribulations knowing that the tribulation brings about perseverance."

Perseverance...the result of pressure.

The pressure of finances...the pressure of difficult circumstances...of sorrow and heartache of children who hurt, children who rebel...of loneliness and realization of having built the ladder of success on the wrong wall. Pressures can produce a spirit that not only passively endures but actively conquers.

"I do not like crisis, but I do like the opportunities they provide." —Lord John Reith

When Beethoven was threatened with deafness, a great loss for a musician, he said: **"I will take life by the throat!"**

Perseverance...out of the battle you can emerge stronger, purer, and most importantly nearer to the heart of God. Are you allowing your fears, your anger, to crush you or crush you closer to the heart of God?

Patience in Greek literally means endurance. It is more than patience; it is submissiveness—there is a note of triumph. It is the ability to bear things in such a triumphant way that it transfigures you. It enables a person to pass the breaking point...not to break...to greet the unseen with a cheer. Countless sufferers found relief from their pain in making their experiences minister to others. They convert their own loss into gain. For example, Joni Erickson Tada, who became a quadriplegic as a result of a diving accident, has been giving a unique ministry to the handicapped all over the world. She lectures and paints with her brush in her teeth. The position of her faith has led to creativeness.

A couple, returning home one day, was greeted by their little daughter who in excitement leaned too far over the stairwell and fell to the hallway floor beneath; consequently, she lay dying at their feet. After the shock of her grief had passed, the mother opened their home to shelter "fallen" girls. As she put it, "I have now no daughter of my own, so I shall be a mother to any girl who needs me." In saving others...she saves herself.

God is not one who stands apart from human suffering even though holding the explanation of it in His hand, but he is the one who comes into it—shares it. This thought, upon which faith could stand in any anguish, is based on the character of God—the passionate, relentless, tender Father.

"Heaven is the place where questions and answers become one." —Eli Wieser

Faith accepts positively...acts creatively...and then acquiesces restfully. Having been active, it becomes passive, leaving its problems and solutions quietly to God.

If men suffer, so Christ did suffer…so we can be whole and complete!

Shalom!

JOY

"If you have no joy in your religion, there's a leak in your Christianity somewhere."
—Billy Sunday

If you try to find enjoyment in controlling things, you will end up in disaster. If you try to find enjoyment in knowledge, you will only increase your capacity for agony as well as distress. The only way you can find relief is by basing your joy in God and…by remembering that **"Man's chief end is to glorify God and enjoy Him forever."** Enjoy Him?

Joy in the Nature of God

Joy is neither happiness nor brightness; joy is literally the nature of God in my blood no matter what happens. The spirit of God will fill us to overflowing if we are careful to keep "in the light." We have no business to be weak in God's strength.

Joy is the great note all through the Bible. We have the notion that joy arises from good spirits or good health, but the miracle of the **joy of God** has nothing to do with a man's life or his circumstances or the condition he is in. Jesus does not come to a man and say "Cheer up." He plants within a man the miracle of the joy of God's own nature. Happiness depends on what happens; joy does not. Remember, Jesus had joy praying "that they might have my joy fulfilled in themselves."

"There may be joy in God when there is little joy ***from*** *God."* —Stephen Charnock

Joy in Circumstances

The miracle of the Christian life is that God can give a person joy in the midst of external misery…joy that gives them power to work until the misery is removed.

Joy is different from happiness, because happiness depends on what happens. Haven't you found there are so many different elements in our circumstances that we cannot control…joy is independent of all of them. The joy of anything lies in fulfilling the purpose of its creation. Jesus Christ's joy is that He fulfilled the design of His Father's will, and my joy is that I fulfill God's design in calling me to be a follower of Him.

Joy in Work

One of the most fantastic stories in Scripture has to with Nehemiah, the general contractor for the rebuilding of the Jerusalem wall. ***"So the wall was finished"*** (Nehemiah 6:15). The impossible was completed in 52 days by a man who cared and dared.

Luke the physician, Paul the tentmaker, Peter the fisherman, Joshua the Chief of Staff, or Gideon the farmer. . . all are men who refused to do things halfway. Whatever their hands found to do, they did it, and they did it with zest. They did it with all their might. In every case, **faithfulness in little...faithfulness in much.** Enthusiasm is infectious! It is impossible to be under the heat of Christianity and come out cold. To be indifferent, unconcerned, or reluctant as a Christian is a contradiction in terms.

Meet the Savior...He will kindle your heart and set you free. When your earthly fire is lit from His divine altar, all things are possible.

"Holy joy is the oil to the wheels of our obedience." —Matthew Henry

As your servants, we are determined to "enjoy Jesus and not endure Christianity." Join us in joy!

—•••—

BOND SERVANT

Why did Paul use the term **"bond servant"** often? He was not masochistic but rather chose this position as a privilege. The Greek word "doulos" comes from the combination of "deo" (to blind) and "leuo" (a servant). Romans 6:19 states that we are "free from sin and enslaved to God." The benefit of this is sanctification now...and eternal life in the future.

A bond slave is one who gives himself up to the will of another (1 Corinthians 7:23). If you knew you had been bought with a price, the precious blood of Christ, wouldn't it be easy to be a slave...one willingly bound to a new Master who has displayed such great love for you?

The great motive of inspirational service is not that God has saved, sanctified, or healed me…all that is a fact. The great motive of service is the realization that **I owe all of my life to the redeeming grace of God.** Therefore, I can choose to be a bond slave of Jesus.

A bond servant was proud of having chosen to serve his master. Once a slave was freed from slavery, he then could choose to continue as a bond servant with his master. As an outward sign of this, he would place his ear against the doorpost of the house and a hole would be nailed in his ear. A ring would then be placed there so all would know he **willingly** chose to be a bond servant. Do you think all these teenagers with rings in their ears know about this?!

Many people are at work for God not because they appreciate His salvation but because they think they should "do something" for other people. Our Lord never called anyone to work for Him because they realized they needed to do so, but only because He has done something for them. The basis of work for God is an extreme appreciation for His salvation. Our Lord told the disciples not to rejoice in successful service but to rejoice because they were rightly related to Him.

If you are devoted to the cause of humanity, you will soon be exhausted and have your heart broken by ingratitude. Jesus healed ten blind men. How many came back to thank him? One. But if the main spring of your service is love for Jesus, you can serve others although they may treat you as a doormat. God wants to use us as He used His own Son. Our call is not to successful service but to faithfulness.

The foundation of faith needs to be drilled deep into the fabric of God's faithfulness. Don't give up—hold on. The trustworthiness of God is ready for every servant's emergencies for when you…

Step out into the darkness…He is the Light.

Move forward…He is the Rock.

Stagger upon your unknown path…He is the Guide.

Waver and doubt…He is the Truth.

> *"All of God's greats have been weak men who did great exploits for God because they reckoned… on His being faithful."* —Hudson Taylor

Where love is…there is no sacrifice. Why not let love flow today by obeying what we know He has already told us to do? **It is a choice! Will you choose?**

—•••—

SOVEREIGNTY AND SEVERE MERCY

An amazing story! Join me as you look at Daniel 4:1-34.

Have you ever thought about a course in "How To Survive in Success and Prosperity"? Success tends to promote a prideful self-sufficiency, rather than a humble gratitude to God. Look at King Nebuchadnezzar as the dream is described and the dream is deciphered by Daniel of Nebuchadnezzar's fame and his fate. Can you imagine what it felt like to go from being the king, one of the most invincible, beautiful, and most powerful kings of that time? He conquered Jerusalem and took Judah into captivity.

Daniel explains the dream. Twelve months later, forgetting that, Neb walks around the city and says, "Look how wonderful I am." Not remembering that he would be reduced for seven years of acting like an animal with claws on his fingers, hair growing on his back, and crawling on all fours. **Think about it!** Have you heard people say God won't force anybody to do anything? God is not involved in the affairs of our secular world? Well, look what happened to Nebuchadnezzar out of his pride. Realize, as I have, God is absolutely sovereign:

> **"God is the absolute and supreme ruler in the universe**
> **over His creation and in all events. God is absolutely free.**
> **He is able to do as He pleases. Always…everywhere**
> **…forever."**

Nebuchadnezzar wrote this story to inform his kingdom of his submission to the one true God as he **"raised his eyes toward Heaven."**

> *"Prosperity knits a person to the world. He feels that he is 'finding his place in it,' where really it is finding its place in him."* —C.S. Lewis

Prosperity is a much harder test to pass than adversity. I've seen it with those who have come out of Residency training and buy the newest of the new Lexus and large houses and have to work hard to pay off debt. One physician said to me, "I let my job eat out the center of my life, leaving me only with the crust."

Do you hide or deny pride? Your self-esteem can assume proper dimension only when your God esteem is high. Let these thoughts wash through you of the blessing of God's sovereignty.

• There is comfort in trials and weakness. 2 Corinthians 1:3, Hebrews 2:18

- You are bathed in His love. Romans 8:37-39, John 17:22-26

- "You cannot thwart His love. You cannot make Him stop loving you."

- Full forgiveness is Sovereign security. Romans 8:31-34, Isaiah 43:25, Hebrews 7:25

The Creator God is involved in the warp and woof of your life. Join me as I fall down to worship…so God will give us the power to rise up…and work.

"Nothing is more insane than human pride. Nothing is more sensible than to praise God."

—•••—

TIME…PRAYER…TIME

God is the Eternal Now. God simply is. Always has been. Never had a beginning. Will never have an end. With God, there is no succession of moments, past or future…only one…Eternal Now.

You and I are not wired to handle a concept like this. We were built to operate within a particular "succession of moments." Anything outside this frame of reference makes us uncomfortable.

"But do not let this one fact escape your notice, beloved, that with the Lord one day is as a thousand years, and a thousand years is as one day." 2 Peter 3:8-9

God chose to know the inexpressible joy He finds in His Son, Jesus, and at the same moment could enter into the horror of that instant when His Son cried, "My God, My God, why have You forsaken me?" He is not disturbed by what seems to us such an impossible paradox.

He is…eternal.

God has chosen to move with us through these successive "moments." He did this with the Israelites as He shared their moments of triumph and joy out of Egypt. He was angered by their moments of stubborn disobedience, and He looked forward with them to the joys of the promised land…and then He grieved when they threw that privilege away through unbelief. He looks forward to our arrival in heaven—He's waiting for it.

What a moment it will be for Him!

How can this be…to see the whole sweep of history at a glance and yet remain intimately involved with the mundane moments of my Friday morning?

Recently, John Martin, a friend, wanted to teach me how to kayak, so we went down the Ocoee River one Saturday. This was the first time for me. It was unfolding moments of adventure, of rapids, of still water, bugs flying across the water, not knowing what was ahead. I rested in the comfort that he had done this many times.

He knew what was ahead. Yet he wanted me, out of his own love for me, to experience the changing complexities of the river as my own experience. He knew what was ahead, but he didn't destroy my joy of facing almost going over at any moment!

God deals with us in the same way, for He is with us in our journey. It is His choice. Tomorrow is tomorrow with God, yesterday is yesterday, today is today, and this moment is His moment; therefore, when we go through times of grief, we have a sympathetic God who identifies with us. When you experience great joy, you have an empathic High Priest who shares your delight. Why has He chosen to move through time with us? It is because He loves us so much.

"A day is like a thousand years." What is God telling us? I believe He wants us to appreciate the value of the moments of our lives. There may be times in our lives when a single day in God's sight is equal to a thousand years of ordinary living. Ironically, the very moments God considers the most valuable…we may consider the most worthless.

"In this world we have tribulation," finding ourselves facing days of great trial…crushing grief…bitter confrontation with the powers of darkness. Oh, how we wish these hours would pass! Our instant prayer becomes, "Lord, get me out of this!"

If we were quiet to listen for God's reply, we might hear Him say, "Wait a minute, this very day in your life is worth a thousand years. Don't rush it!" Think of Stephen. There was "one" day…a day when Stephen, preaching his heart out, met a wall of hate and hail of stones. "Look," he said, "I see heaven open and the Son of Man standing on the right hand of God!" The enraged mob smashed his body with every rock they could grab, with him slumping to the ground, asking for mercy for them. His "one" day was hardly more than a few minutes, yet in God's eyes was worth a lifetime.

When are you most fully alive? It's when your life seems most threatened…when life by all appearances is being lost…when we cry out, "Lord! I am losing it!" God answers, "Oh, no, my child. These moments of Ruthless Trust are more precious to Me than hours or weeks of plain existing. These moments are your fullness of life."

Do you feel…

you are hurting because your deferred gratification caused you to miss out on the fullness of life?

Do you feel…

loneliness while others seem surrounded by close friends or others are so robust and you're in pain?

Do you feel…

rejected while others received praise, living in unceasing pain while others relax in comfort?

And, you say it isn't fair! Why have the days slipped by that could have been so full of happiness? What have I done to deserve this? Please…please grasp what Paul says:

"Our light affliction is but for a moment working for us far more exceedingly an eternal weight of glory." 2 Corinthians 4:17

Paul, when he was stoned, didn't look to have "light affliction" to me.

But, Paul had found out that when you weigh your troubles, it all depends on what you place on the opposite side of the scale. To put all your heartaches, losses, and disappointments on one side makes them seem unbearable…until you place the "eternal weight of glory" on the other. Suddenly, heavy becomes light, when weighed against the eternal delight.

As a wonderful physician let us stay at their home in North Carolina, I saw trees that may have been a hundred or a thousand years old. I compared my short life and said, "It's not fair, God. You've mixed the priorities up somehow." Then I realized that long after these trees have fallen to dust that I will still be young, tasting forever of the "tree of life." As I look in the mirror, I feel like I'm getting old. My old tent has some lines, wrinkles, and other signs of wear…but so what! God says I'm going to be young forever!

What an inexpressible joy to be God's new creation, built for eternity…His workmanship. And while we live here on this earth, He's using "time"—those sometimes painful sequences of "moments"—to add facets to the spiritual diamond that is you and me. . . so that we will be able to more perfectly reflect His beauty and glory, now and throughout eternity. When God thinks I'm ready, He's going to take that diamond to heaven to flash, to sparkle forever, not in itself but in the reflection of the glory of God in the face of Christ.

How much time do you want with God? Whose terms do you want that "time" on? Do you incorporate prayer into your time? Live in the present moment…live in the now…in prayer.

BITTERSWEET

Moses, when faced with a burning bush and the call of God, said, "Here I am, Lord; send Aaron!" Moses eventually obeyed God's call, leading the children of Israel out of Egypt. He experienced the miraculous event of the Red Sea being parted for some 750,000 Israelites and the drowning of the Egyptians in the flood waters. After a three-day journey through the wilderness of Thur, they found the water. They grumbled. How shall we drink?

> ***Then he cried out to the Lord and the Lord showed him a tree; and he threw it into the waters, and the waters became sweet. There he made for them a statue and regulation and there He tested them.***
> Exodus 15:25

Three long days...the desert sun glared, baking the moisture from their bodies. As their hearts and bodies grew weak from the sweltering heat, they came to a clear pool of sparkling water. Dismay! Stooping to drink, they discovered the water was bitter. They reasoned, "We were delivered from oppression only to die of exposure and dehydration." Is God cruel? No, in His love He was preparing to unveil a truth. It goes far deeper than supplying bodily needs. He was offering the Israelites...and us...a glimpse through the desert to His heart of love.

A tree...If they were expecting something as dramatic as the parting of the sea, they were sorely disappointed. Moses' simple act of obedience—throwing a tree into the bitter waters—was all that was needed. Instantly bitterness gave way to sweetness. God was teaching His children to trust. The power that brought them out of Egypt was the same power that would provide for their needs each day.

The tree—the agent of God's delivering power—foreshadowed the cross of Jesus Christ.

There are no impossibilities with God—only opportunities to make the bitter become sweet.

Jesus on the cross openly destroyed Satan's authority. Yet, when we are faced with the appearance of this toothless lion, how often we lose our composure. A third-year UAB medical student reported that the students in Philadelphia with the Summer Medical Project are facing opposition from people with obvious demonic influence. What do we do? **When trouble comes our way we throw in the tree;** i.e., we apply the cross to the situation. However, the cross is not only to be applied but to be experienced. The cross of Christ—divinity and humanity—met where the Lamb's blood flowed, where the Vine was wounded for our grafting in. His power...His life. . . His spirit flow into us in direct proportion to our experience of His cross. As this deepens our knowledge of God, then all of our bitter waters will become sweet.

The wilderness has the ability to burn through the smoothest and most polished veneer to reveal the innermost nature of a person. God wants His children to be stripped of every vain encumbrance so that we may trust His love. **"He exposes our weakness so that He might reveal His strength."**

Was God being callous? No, He saw the needs of the children. He provided. Changes are coming fast in medicine and dentistry. OSHA complaint forms...Obamacare. The dental hygienist we trained was just hired by my competitor. Medicaid payments are down. The willingness (to go to the cross) is painful and often a lonely experience...but it is an essential step enabling us to enjoy a divine union and a rich fellowship with Jesus Christ our Lord.

Are you stranded in a spiritual wilderness without a compass, comfort, or companion? Have emotions erupted in frustration...anger...and fear? If so, take heart—deserts give you a new understanding, an oasis in God!

> *"And he said, 'If you will give earnest heed to the voice of the Lord your God and do what is right in His sight and give ear to His commandments, keep all His statues, I will put none of these diseases on you which I have put on the Egyptians, for I, the Lord, am your healer."* Exodus 15:26

This is the branch that was thrown in to make your wilderness experience bittersweet. After the branch comes blessings.

I, the Lord, am your healer.

---•••---

IDOLATRY AND WORSHIP

People must worship…it's our nature. It's built in. If we don't worship the one true God, the heart will invent its own god! Excessive love for anything is a mockery of God's first commandment: "Thou shalt have no other gods before Me."

> ***"See now…that I am He and…there is no god beside me. It is I who put to death and give life, I have wounded and it is I who heal and there is no one who can deliver from My hand."*** Deuteronomy 32:9

God has sovereign sway over all events. Every situation is known to Him. Sickness, financial setbacks, family misunderstandings, life's darkest hours

…all these happen within the framework of His purposes. No matter what the predicament, God is still God!

Any object that produces passionate devotion is an imposter leading to idolatry. We laugh at those in the Old Testament who would take a tree, carve it to make an idol, and then bow down before it. But, if we love…

Success…
Ambition…
Prominence…
Possessions…

We have enthroned an idol in our heart. How do you define idolatry? When we long for what we dare not do, hunger after what we must not have, and lust for what we should not love, this is the start of idolatry.

Our attitude toward our circumstances determines our victory or defeat. The same wind that carries one ship into the port will dash another upon the rocks.

> *"Happy is he whose circumstances suit his temper; but he is more excellent who can suit his temper to any circumstance."* —David Hume

Circumstances are the refining pot. Through trials and temptations, the object of our worship is revealed. Job learned firsthand (and so must we) that before the butterfly there is a struggle in the cocoon. There is no feast without a sacrifice. Job's character was matured by trials. He was strengthened by discipline. He was enriched by disappointments.

How do we worship God? Isn't worship a love offering from the depths of our innermost being…expressing an intense sense of the worth-ship of a Holy, Awesome God? It is presenting back to God the love that He "shed abroad" in our own hearts.

WORSHIP…WAITING…WORK…They were always together in the life of Jesus. He "worshipped" the Father. He "waited" for His direction. He "worked the works of Him who sent Him." **Men must worship something.** It is our nature.

"What you bend your knee to is what you worship."

Where your treasure is there your heart is also. Where is your treasure? **What do you worship?** Is it the one true God, or is it a substitute?

—•••—

THE FRUIT OF JOY

How do you handle emotions? God created us with emotions so that we might be able to enjoy Him and His creation. Do you consider your feelings as a bother, a hindrance to living a vital life of faith? God gave us emotions so that we might live a wholesome life. God Himself is an emotional being who expresses a range of emotions such as anger… pleasure…compassion. How do we achieve emotional wholeness?

We can't expect a life without emotional turbulence, but there can be emotional healing even with ups and downs of test schedules and clinicals. Do you manage your emotions, or do they manage you?

Joy is the flag flown from the castle of the heart when the king is in residence there.

**Joy is a fruit of the spirit. It comes when we accept death to our plans and ambitions and receive what Christ has for us. The issue is self-rule versus Christ-rule.

** Many people seek happiness and never find it because it's not found when you seek it directly. Happiness is part of the blessing that comes from doing the will of God.

** John the Baptist shows us joy. The friend of the bridegroom was responsible to bring the bride to the bridegroom and after introducing them in the marriage ceremony, the friend stepped quietly away. In John 3:29 John the Baptist used this custom as an illustration of his relationship to Jesus Christ. His responsibility was to introduce people to the Bridegroom and then fade into the background. It was this that completed John's joy.

Have you introduced your patients, family, and colleagues to your Bridegroom Jesus?

Today there's much advice on how to find lasting happiness...well-defined goals such as self-fulfillment, a challenging career, or making money. At the root, these recommendations can be sinful! Our goal should be what John summarized in John 3:30: ***"He must increase...but I must decrease."***

Let's remember that the joy of the Holy Spirit does not come by seeking self-fulfillment; it comes by seeking Christ's fulfillment.

What God enjoys:
...salvation of people brings compelling joy (Luke 15:32),
...righteousness living by believers (Proverbs 11:20),
...contemplating creation (Psalm 104:31).

What do people enjoy? The same as above.
It is impossible to be under the heart of Christianity and come out cold
...indifferent...unconcerned.

Experience joy by...
...an acceptance of the greatness of God,
...a glow of emotion arising from that knowledge,
...a consciousness of obligation to spread the Word!

True **joy** comes when we en**joy** Christ.

—•••—

PROVIDENCE

"To everything there is a season, and a time for every purpose under heaven, a time to be born. . . I know that whatever God does it endures forever; nothing can be added to it nor anything taken from it and God does it so that man will hear Him—know that He is—revere and worship Him." Ecclesiastes 3:1, 14

There are 14 maxims that cover all the events that come into our lives in Ecclesiastes 3:2-8. **Read the list!** Everything is covered...from industrial relations to human labor, social and business practices, human feelings and public service, plus life and death, fun and sorrow, ending with the dilemma of war and peace. As my friend Rev. Don Tabb of the Chapel on the Campus used to say...

"Our disappointments are often God's appointments."

Be sure...nothing just happens to the child of God. There are no mere accidents in your life. In this world of perpetual change (healthcare legislation), fluctuating events (technology), and shifting circumstances (where will I practice?), it's great to have a stable center that says, "Our times are in His hands" (Psalm 31:15), while the wheels of Providence roll along the highway of Divine Purpose. Time is nothing to God.

Is God Sovereign? Since He is, that means every tear, every sorrow, every misfortune, every calamity, every catastrophe such as hurricanes, tornados, famines, freezes, depression and plagues, sickness and pain, disappointments and even death..."all things. . . work together, cooperate, move in mighty teamwork—for good to them that love God."

Watch God's way in your life. You will find He is developing you as he does the trees and flowers, a deep silent working of the creative God. **"Consider the lilies of the field."** A lily is not always in the sunshine; for the greatest part of the year it is in the dark. They grow in the dark...and for a short time in the light they are radiantly beautiful and sweet.

"We can never be lilies in the garden...
unless we spend time as bulbs in the dark."

That is how to grow in the grace and in the providence of God.

What are the lessons for our hearts from Solomon's wisdom? **First,** there is no fatalism. **Secondly,** man's confidence must be based upon practical dependence on God. **Thirdly,** the God who is neither fickle nor short-sighted is intensely interested in you! Believers are the Father's gifts to Jesus (See John 17:2, 6, 9, 11-12) just as Jesus is the Father's love gift to us (John 3:16).

Because we are God's gift to Jesus, we can allow the human clay that's frail and weak, that breaks and comes unglued very easily, to be the vessel that contains the Creator Jesus. "But, Earle, isn't that hard to believe when you look at political trends, media influence, degenerated morals, and insecurity of lost jobs?" Medical graduates used to feel the future was certain; now so many that are already practicing medicine feel uncertain of the future! **Maybe it means we will have to trust God today.** Risky? Let's support and encourage each other in Jesus to be secure in our insecurity…to be a lily waiting for the time that God will have us bloom…and then bloom where we are planted.

Is it true that our disappointments are God's appointments? There is a time for…

———•••———

FACES

The face of Jesus Christ must have been very beautiful, since His life was spotless and pure. The thoughts of a person make the face. It is sin that disfigures the human countenance. We cannot hide our inner life from man's eyes. What goes on in the depths of our soul comes up to the surface of our face!

If you are discontented, it will be revealed in your features. If you have bitter thoughts in your heart, it will write its hard lines on your countenance. If you think kindly thoughts and peaceful thoughts, on your face will come gentleness, kindness, and peace. If you keep love in your heart, amid all tests and irritations, your face will shine with love. A principle…

"Beautiful thoughts make a beautiful soul, and a beautiful soul makes a beautiful face."

"But we all, with unveiled face beholding as in a mirror the glory of the Lord, are being transformed into the same image from glory to glory, just as from the Lord the Spirit." 2 Corinthians 4:18

Jesus' face was transfigured, shining as the sun, because of the glory within. Moses' face shone brightly when he had been long in communion with God on the Mount. Stephen's face shone as he saw the face of Jesus before he was stoned to death, revealing the peace, quiet, and joy that dwelt within.

Where do we find the beauty of the glory of the face of Christ? A monk who had a great desire to see Christ fled to a monastery where he could read, meditate, and pray, hoping there to view the **face of Jesus.** Days were spent in penance, nights in prayer. One morning he heard a voice that seemed to say today he would see Jesus' face. In the midst of his seeking, a gentle tap at his door revealed a child pleading to be taken in to be sheltered and fed. Being barefoot and scantily clothed and having a thin body revealed her needs. But the monk was busy with his devotions and had no time for others with their needs. Why was the vision so delayed? Christ had come. . . in the child he had not welcomed but sent away.

If we are to see the **face** of Jesus, we must look for Him in the common ways. The pages of Scripture are the source for seeing the reflected face of Christ. As we ponder these pages, we will find ourselves being "transformed from glory to glory."

The Book of Revelation says of the redeemed, "They shall see His face." No veils, no shadows; **we shall see Him as He is...face to face.**

———•••———

BRING A GIFT

Just imagine it...The God of creation had to borrow a donkey! Without a doubt, the happiest man on the first Palm Sunday was the one who loaned his donkey to Christ. The King of Kings had to borrow a donkey and a colt for His ride into town! The need of the hour was transportation, and a poor peasant servant was the source of supply.

It is the story of God commandeering through the reality of Grace. People didn't have to...no strong arm was used...they gave freely. It was a...

> borrowed stable at birth,
> > a little boy's lunch to feed thousands,
> > > a borrowed tomb to bury Christ in.

Christ cannot ride in royalty without you. Nothing, absolutely nothing can be added to the cross, but its application is dependent upon man's response.

You are God's tool.

You and yours are the vehicle to reach your world.

"Every man in Israel shall appear before the Lord your God three times a year at the Sanctuary, and on each of these occasions...bring a

gift to the Lord...give as you are able...according as the Lord has bless-ed you." Deuteronomy 16:16-17

"**Bring** a gift...**give** as able...**according** to as you're blessed"...all things are His: donkeys, education degrees, gold, gifts, talents, treasures, Life. Note: He has given us temporary possession of them. We are stewards to manage things that are Someone Else's. They are given to us to make them His!

"What I have grabbed I have lost.
What I give I have received!"

The donkey came back to the servant more precious, more valuable, for the King of Kings had considered to use it. Premise: You lose nothing when that which you have is pressed into the service for His Glory.

Wealthy Job was bankrupt. After carefully analyzing the situation, although complete-ly baffled by the circumstances, Job asked to be weighted in the balance of moral integ-rity.

"If I have put my trust in money, if my happiness depends on wealth, if I have done such things...it would mean that I denied the God of heaven." Job 31:24-28

Have I put my trust in money? Have I been spending upon wealth? Until you put yourself in God's work, you will never realize a payoff. Do not try to get your paycheck to do what you are unwilling to perform. God does not need your stocks or money, but **He does need you!** Sometimes...sometimes...He will strip you to find out who is holding what!

Obedience loosens the hands that clothe our possessions. Love unlocks funds for His disposal. **Joyfully** the servant released what he had. Without debate...without delay... respond to God's desire. **Give Him the donkey!**

"Everyone must make up his own mind as to how much he should give. Do not force anyone to give more than he really wants to...for cheerful givers are the ones God prizes." 2 Corinthians 9:7

"**Bring** a gift...**give** as able...**according** to as you're blessed."

———●●●———

GUILT OF SIN…GRACE OF GOD

God has created us to be dependent. We have sought to be independent. That is idolatry…pride.

"Sin…always takes from you more than you wanted to give…always keeps you much longer than you wanted to stay…will always cost you much more than you want to pay."
—Lee Savage, Camp Utopia Metro Church of God

Why mention sin? Isn't that negative? Tell me of the love of God! Physicians are negative in that they have to "hurt to help." When a patient has water on the knee, the physician does not compliment them on how wonderful all the rest of the body is, but they lance the knee. The patient cries out, "If you love me, why do you hurt me?" It is because the physician loves the patient. He has to hurt to help. Have you faced the root of sin and the fantastic forgiveness found in the grace of God?

Sin makes you co-dependent—perfectionism, workaholism, alcoholism, drugs, success, never making mistakes… all kinds of means of taking opportunity to be independent of God's power.

We all know what it is to be troubled, to have a restless inner life, to be haunted by the feeling that we were made for something better, but have not quite attained to it. Memory of past stings, outbursts of rage, jealousy, envy all leave us troubled. For some, the intensity of the negative feelings is so strong that their entire life seems to be nothing but a profound alienation from nature, man, and ultimately God.

The Roman philosopher Seneca knew of this haunting of the conscience:

"Sin can be well-guarded, but free from anxiety, it cannot be. We are all sinful; **therefore, whatever we blame in another, we shall find in our own bosoms."**

You can compromise your conscience, but you will find that your conscience will not finally compromise with you. It is God's point of contact to convict us, to recognize our responsibility for them, and most importantly, ultimately to show us our need for His forgiveness.

We are all tied up with seeking to impress people and have good feelings about ourselves, when in reality we do not please people all that much, and certainly, we do not feel good about ourselves. Man's struggle with guilt—his lack of assurance his sins are forgiven, even among Christians—often comes after use of religious activity to keep God at a distance.

What is God's answer to a troubled conscience? His solution? God Almighty took the problem of the sin of the world on His own shoulders. It made Him stoop. The Bible begins with the finished work of Christ to make the righteousness of Christ your foundation for the assurance of your forgiveness. God is perfectly satisfied with Christ's sacrifice of His own precious blood. He is our advocate, not presenting the merits of our feeble "good works" but His perfect work. Our acceptance of God does not depend upon our good or bad behavior or even upon feelings about ourselves, but upon Christ alone. **We bring to Him only our unlimited need, and He brings to us His unlimited forgiveness.**

> *"Great peace have they who love Your law, and nothing can make them stumble."* Psalm 119:165

The sadness of not being perfect and the discovery that you are sinful is a feeling so human. Focus your vision outside yourself on the beauty, graciousness, and compassion of Jesus Christ. The pure of heart praise Him from sunrise to sundown, even when they feel broken, feeble, distracted, insecure, and uncertain. They are able to release it into His peace.

A heart like that is stripped of self and filled with the fullness of God. **Jesus is Lord. That suffices.**

———•••———

I AM WHO I AM

Whom do you trust?

> The one you know the best.
> The one you know who loves you the most.

The bedrock on which to build trust is…who God is. Moses found this out from the burning bush when he asks by what name he was being sent to Egypt.

> ***And God said to Moses, "I am…who I am has sent me to you."***
> Exodus 3:14

I AM

"Am" is the first-person present tense of the verb "to be." He was and will be what He is…eternally present. Pharaoh discovered in the plagues God was the God of power… of justice…of punishing wrath. God was to Pharaoh "what HE IS."

To Israel, God was "faithfulness"…"compassion" by giving manna and water from the Rock…"wisdom" in the giving of the Law…"grace" at the brazen altar…"patience" in 40 years of wandering.

Jesus said of God, "Now my heart is troubled, and what shall I say? 'Father, save me from this hour'? No, it was for this very reason I came to this hour. Father, glorify your name!" Then a voice came from heaven, "I have glorified it, and will glorify your name." John 12:27-28

'This hour' was the cross. He cried out "Let this cup pass from me!" Not because of fear of pain but because He knew that at the moment, He "became sin" and His "I AM" Father would become His Judge. You who have always been "love" to me will instead become infinite wrath and eternal justice. Sin separates! He took the hits!

YOU WILL BE TO ME WHAT YOU ARE.

For you and me…Because of Jesus, the "I AM" FREES us from wrath!

> ***"For God has not destined us for wrath but for obtaining salvation through our Lord Jesus Christ."*** 1 Thessalonians 5:9

God is now free to be to us…
>Everything that He is…without wrath.
>In my weakness, He will be omnipotence.
>In my loneliness, He will be omnipresent.
>In my sorrow, He will be joy.
>In my brokenness, He will be my healer.

If you know the "I AM," you will trust.

GOD is what He promises…His name to be!

"I AM"

— •••

LITTLE THINGS

The older I get, the **"little things"** seem to become "big things." **"Little things"** mean a lot. One drop of poison in the glass…one small match lit in a forest…one rotten apple in the crate. Little things may seem like insignificant habits or minor sins or unnoticed traits that might be in the hidden corners of our life. It is not enough that we be "sincere" but we must also be "without offense."

> *"Dead flies cause the ointment of the perfume to putrefy and send forth a vile odor. So does a 'little' folly in him who is valued for wisdom outweigh wisdom and honor."* Ecclesiastes 10:1

Expensive ointment plus a dead insect equals a big stink! We need to be so careful not to spoil the fragrance of the ointments of our testimony by preaching against the big sins… murder, social injustice, or adultery…but practice a lifestyle of "the lustful eye, the hasty word, the irritable temper, the rudeness of our behavior, occasional slip of the tongue."

"He who is a Christian in **small things** is not a small Christian."

…Ananias and Sapphira withheld just a "minimum" amount of their gift.
…Moses in anger struck the rock, which seemed to be such a "small" thing.
…Samson told Delilah a "harmless" secret he had with God.
…Lot's wife took a "quick" glance back toward Sodom.
…King David took just a "little" look at Bathsheba on the roof bathing.

These men and women had a tremendous reputation. . . until the "dead flies" got into the ointment of their lives. Perfumes were commonly kept in sealed alabaster jars under the watchful eye of the perfumer. How would bugs ever get in the vat? One answer… carelessness. The cover wasn't replaced. Neglect in the caring allowed dead flies to drop in the jar. At first it wasn't noticed, but under the heat and pressure of daily living… there rose a mighty stink!

Can you be too scrupulous? In this day of relativity and situational ethics, you just can't afford to make exceptions on divine requirements. If you desire to move upward and forward don't be flexible with your soul. **Leave the lid off of your thought life and the lustful flies will start the mental rot.** Neglect the sealing of your heart to impure motives and desires and it won't be long before the aroma is sickening. Plug the hole in the dike of your personal life by daily devotions with the Abba Father, the Daddy of your life. Sit, laugh, cry with Him. His face is grace. King Solomon found that his life was fouled up by sin and folly; how he wishes those "dead flies" had never gotten in.

The **"little things"** of your life can be confronted by your initiating accountability to friends, your spouse, or a body of believers. Who do you have that you expect will inspect…the little things?

"Little things" mean a lot. A lot to Jesus…a lot to you…a great deal to your children. Let the perfume of your life be a sweet-smelling sacrifice to Jesus in every place.

Keep the dead flies out!

———•••———

REJECTION

Have you ever thought about the fact that God the Father might feel like a rejected parent?

Many of us know how it feels to have been rejected as a child.

Children who have been rejected by one of their parents feel abandonment…a lack of acceptance. Maybe the parent didn't show up at the dance recital or cheer them on at the game or even verbally or physically abused them. Children suffering this emotional baggage of lack of acceptance feel anger, repress it…but it shows up when they get married.

Circumstances of life reveal a person's spirit, not cause it. —Dr. Henry Brandt

But…what about God?

> **"How often I wanted to gather your children together the way a hen gathers her chicks under her wings and you were unwilling."**
> Matthew 23:37

> **"The younger son gathered everything together and went on a journey to the far country, and there he squandered his estate with loose living."** Luke 15:13

He has certainly not rejected us. He has given His son, Jesus, to heal the broken heart, to be made sin for us, and to give us His very own righteousness. He has accepted us fully as His children because of what Jesus did for us.

No, He has not rejected us!

But, we can reject Him...does He feel rejected?

Does He know what it is like to have children who don't behave as they should? Does He know what it is like to feel the heartache that only children can give their parents? Does He feel the pain of children...that have gone to the far country simply to get away from home?

Sure, He does. He is our Abba! Father! A very patient one. Jesus said...

> *"For we do not have a High Priest who cannot sympathize with our weakness, but one who has been tempted in all things as we are yet without sin."* Hebrews 4:15

The Living Solution!

The ultimate pain, the ultimate rejection...Christ suffered in our place on the brutal cross.

> *"How much more will the blood of Christ who through the eternal Spirit offered Himself without blemish to God cleanse your conscience from dead works...to serve a living God."* Hebrews 9:14

He was rejected. You are totally accepted.

Think about it!

—•••—

SHELTER

Where do you turn when the bottom drops out of your life? Or when you are embarrassed, like:

...your salary just got cut.

...your mate is talking separation or divorce.

...your daughter has run away...is she pregnant?

What do you need when circumstances threaten to engulf your life with pain and confusion?

You need a "shelter." A listener. Where do you find encouragement?

Bruised by adversity, the pain of his children…struggling David writes:

> *"In you, O Lord, I have taken refuge; let me never be put to shame; deliver me in your righteousness. Turn your ear to me, come quickly to my rescue; be my rock of refuge."* Psalm 31:1-2

Wounded in spirit and weakening in strength, David cries for a "refuge"…a protected place of safety, security. **David found it in the Lord!**

Why the need? Because…

We are in distress and sorrow overwhelms us…

"My eyes grow weak…my life is consumed by anguish" (v. 9-10).

Sorrow weighs down…the serpent of despair slithers silently through the soul's back door.

Depression is…doubting God cares, doubting He's even here…debilitating gloom makes choices hard.

Why the need? Because…

We are surrounded by assaults from culture, family, or friends.

> *"Because of all my enemies, I am the utter contempt of my neighbors; those who see me on the street flee from me. I am forgotten by them as though I were dead; I have become like broken pottery. For I hear the slander of many; they conspire against me."* Psalm 31:11-13

Gossip shoves us to the edge of despair, feeling contempt…forgotten…slandered.

What helps? Discouraged people don't need critics or guilt piled on them. We hurt enough already. We need encouragement…a place to hide…to heal

…a refuge.

Can you find someone? Someone who is caring…confident? Why not slip into the shelter David found?

> *"But as for me, I trust in Thee, O Lord. My times are in Thy hand. Save me in Thy lovingkindness, Hide in the secret place, Keep me secretly in a shelter. Be strong…let your heart take courage, all you who hope in the Lord."* Psalm 31:14-24

Don't throw in the towel or allow despair to roll over your soul like a cold fog. Don't faint in the race…have ruthless trust. Believe to see. When all props are gone, He will strengthen your heart.

—•••—

THANKSGIVING IN THE MIDST

"This way of seeing our Father in everything makes life one long thanksgiving and gives a rest of heart, and, more than that, a gayety of spirit, that is unspeakable." —Hannah Whitall Smith

"As I look back over fifty years of ministry, I recall innumerable tests, trials, and times of crushing pain, but through it all, the Lord has proven faithful, loving, and totally true to all his promises." —David Wilkerson

"In Everything Give Thanks"

A verse so familiar we recite it almost without thinking as an encouragement to one another in our everyday walk.

However, like a woodman's ax, the reality of life has a way of splitting "everything" into opposing halves.

Good and bad.

Pleasure and pain.

Joys and sorrow.

The front half of the "everything" is easy. Thankful for the birth of a child. For great health. Family. A good job.

The backside of the "everything" is more difficult. The death of a loved one. Cancer. Divorce. A job lost. The empty chair at the head of the table from which Dad said the Thanksgiving blessing just last year.

It's hard to get our hearts and emotions around thanking God for the dark days, for pain, or overwhelming loss.

What's interesting is that our Father does not ask us to. He asks us in 1 Thessalonians 5:18 to be thankful "in" the midst of those things.

Consider the life of Jeremiah. His autobiography recorded in Lamentations chapter 3 paints a dismal portrait of his journey.

Affliction. Darkness. Flesh wasting away. Broken bones. Bitterness. Hardship. Chains. Crooked paths. Bears. Lions. Arrows. Mocking. Rejection.

Reflecting on all of this, Jeremiah bemoans, *"I well remember them, and my soul is downcast within me"* (Lamentations 3:20).

Too often, the tapestries of our own lives have the same threads woven through them.

But, in the midst of despair, Hope always emerges. Jeremiah calls to mind an eternal truth upon which all thanksgiving has its foundation: *"The steadfast love of the Lord never ceases; His mercies never come to an end"* (v.22).

Every trial that enters your life comes through the doorway of the steadfast love of the Lord. It involves love that emanates from our eternally wise Father. *"It is He who made the earth by His power, who established the world by His wisdom"* (Jeremiah 10:12). Isaiah adds that the Lord of Hosts is *"wonderful in counsel and excellent in wisdom"* (Isaiah 28:29).

God is infinitely wise. His steadfast love endures forever. Separate truths, which are inseparable.

And they are truths that transform trials into thanksgiving.

When life is not the way it is supposed to be, when the wheels come off…when looking up is the only choice you have, because you are flat on your back…be thankful.

Be thankful that God is infinitely wise. Be thankful that His steadfast love never ceases and endures forever.

In the midst of everything, give thanks. It will turn your life around.

And your Thanksgiving.

TIME

The Christian life matures and becomes fruitful by the principle of growth of which so much **time** is a necessity. A. H. Strong related a story: A student asked the president of his school if he could take a shorter course than the one described. "Oh yes," replied the president, "but it depends on what you want to be. When God wants to make an oak, He takes 100 years, when He wants to make a squash He takes 6 months." God does not hurry in His development of our Christian life. He is working from and for eternity! Look at Ecclesiastes 3:

"(v. 1) For everything there is a season, and a **time** for every matter under heaven... (v. 5-7) a **time** to embrace, and a **time** to refrain from embracing; a **time** to seek, and a **time** to lose; a **time** to keep, and a **time** to cast away; a **time** to tear, and a **time** to sew; a **time** to keep silence, and a **time** to speak..."

Have you questioned how to use your **time?** Have you ever just wanted to find the time to "be still and know that I am God"? How difficult it is to learn the lesson that there is a time to hurry and a time to slow down. A time for noise and a time for silence. A time to speak and a time to listen.

If you will schedule a time of silence at the beginning of each day, you will find peace, quiet, and assurance. However, this takes time...time alone with God in personal devotions. Such silence and quietness are one's greatest need.

"Time out with God can be a thrilling or a quivering experience."

Our concept of time has us attempting to get each new day off to a "fast start." Residents come out of their beds like a sprinter from a starting block. Doctors start the day with a bang! They never dare let down until they drop like a limp noodle at night—exhausted and completely frustrated by the mad whirl of fascinating responsibilities.

A wise person sets a pace. The first hour is for warming up the motor, setting your vision, preparing your life.

> Fresh for the day
>> First with God
>>> Quietness. . . that quickens.

Since it is so true in medicine we have "permanent emergencies," shouldn't we build into our life time that will prepare us for the battle? Can you afford a few minutes each day for God? You can't afford not to.

"But the one listening to me will dwell secure, will be quiet without dread of calamity." Proverbs 1:33

Ask yourself the question "What do I want to do?" and look at how you use your **time**...that will tell you what you want to do.

BIOGRAPHY

———•••———

Conrad Earle Carpenter was born in Birmingham, Alabama. While being raised in Birmingham, he graduated from the University of Alabama with a B.S. in Business. After serving a stint in the Army, Earle began working for the family business, Carpenter Oak Flooring Company. Not long after this he was called into working as a mortgage banker. His life dramatically changed on Aug 24, 1962, when he married the love of his life, the former Judy Spears.

During their second year of marriage Judy trusted Jesus Christ as her Savior. Even though Earle was a deacon in his church, he saw the reality of Jesus in Judy's life and he, in turn, gave his life to the Lord. In 1967 Earle went on staff with Campus Crusade for Christ and worked as an assistant to Bill Bright. Following this he was on Campus Crusade staff at LSU for five years. He attended Dallas Theological Seminary and graduated with a Masters of Divinity in 1979. Earle and Judy served SMU for three years.

In 1982 a group of physicians and dentists from Birmingham asked Earle to come begin a ministry to doctors in the local community. Later that year in conjunction with Briarwood Presbyterian Church, he founded and directed the Christian Medical Ministry of Alabama for 20 years. He continued to serve CMMA until 2012, when he fully retired to be with Judy. They have two children (Missy and Conrad) and two grandchildren (Julien and Kayin).